The GM MOTORAMA
Dream Cars of the Fifties

MW00561128

Bruce Berghoff

Motorbooks International
Publishers & Wholesalers

Author's Dedication
To Nancy—a butterfly who flew with eagles.

First published in 1995 by Motorbooks International Publishers & Wholesalers, 729 Prospect Avenue, PO Box 1, Osceola, WI 54020-0001 USA

Motorbooks International books are also available at discounts in bulk quantity for industrial or sales-promotional use. For details write to Special Sales Manager at the Publisher's address

Library of Congress Cataloging-in-Publication Data

Berghoff, Bruce.
    The GM Motorama dream cars of the fifties / Bruce Berghoff.
            p. cm.
    Includes index.
    ISBN 0-7603-0053-4 (pbk.)
    1. General Motors Corporation--Exhibitions. 2. Experimental automobiles--United States--History. I. Title.
    TL7.U62N483   1995
    659.1 '52--dc20   95-44653

On the front cover: Pontiac's Club de Mer show car occupies the foreground and the 1961 New York Motorama provides the back drop. *Courtesy General Motors*

On the back cover: Top: 1956 Motorama, Miami, Florida. Several dream cars are visible in this shot including the Corvette Impala, Buick Centurion, Pontiac Club de Mer, and Firebird II. *Bottom:* 1953 Le Sabre dream car.

Printed and bound in the United States of America

Contents

Acknowledgments

Having half a lifetime of auto show experience as a designer, production expediter, road show supervisor, display building company owner, and finally, as a specialty show consultant for the Specialty Equipment Market Association (SEMA) was not enough to get me started as an author.

Several years of prompting from my daughter Kathy and wife Pat, plus numerous comments from author Tony Thacker on how simple it was, finally got this book rolling.

But that, I was to find out, was only the beginning. It still took conversations with Anne DeCamillo, Don Far, Peter Fuller, Sr., Chuck Jordan, Lon Keathley, Gerry Russello, and Cap Stubbs, plus the assistance of Tony Ciminera, Bob Eng, Larry Gustin, Don Keefe, Larry Kinsel, Mary Reed, Bill Warner, Sky Van Duyne, John Gunnell, Wes Yocum, Kathy Berghoff, Bill Berghoff, Jim Preib, and Roxanne Gilbert.

To all of you I extend a big thanks.

—Bruce Berghoff, Arcadia, Michigan

Introduction

I should have known from the first day I went to work for H. B. "Cap" Stubbs in 1955 that this was going to be the beginning of an unforgettable adventure. A journey that would open the door to meeting and working with hundreds of people responsible for conceiving and building the GM Motorama Shows and its Dream Cars. A trip that would last eight years and at the end would see the demise of the automotive world's "Greatest Show on Earth."

From the late 1940s through the early 1960s GM's almost annual Motorama presentations grew in size, entertainment value, and cost . . . especially *cost*. The show decor developed along the lines of contemporary U.S. passenger cars . . . lots of glitz. More was better. Voluptuous curves, plush upholstery, gaudy colors, and acres of chrome became the norm.

People lined up for miles, and hours, to view some of the same cars that had been in their local dealer's showrooms for months. But the difference was the show. The plush carpets and plants, the elaborate costumes and lighting, the dancing girls and boys . . . and the Dream Cars.

Here is the story of the shows, the cars, and some of the people that played a part of automotive history.

CHAPTER 1

IN THE BEGINNING

Merchandising automobiles with fanfare and class might not have been originated by General Motors (GM) Corporation, but GM certainly went a long way toward refining the process.

Beginning with GM's "Industrialist's Luncheons" staged at New York's Waldorf Astoria annually during the 1930s and 1940s, GM showed the auto industry how to get the attention of key movers and shakers from New York's banking and financial centers. By staging a selection of top-end products from each GM automotive division in the elegant Grand Ballroom of the Waldorf, enhanced with carefully coordinated decorations, GM began a tradition that was to culminate with the GM Motorama extravaganzas of the 1950s and early 1960s.

General Motors not only laid the ground work for the Motorama shows in the 1930s and 1940s, it also built the car that has become known as the inspiration for the Dream Cars of the 1950s.

Identified only as the "Y-Job," this experimental Buick, started in 1938, was not revealed to the public until 1940. Directed by Harley Earl, head of GM's styling section, the Y-Job was custom built on a 1937 Buick chassis stretched to almost twenty feet in length to create the proper proportion desired by Mr. Earl,

Incorporated in its ultra-rounded body were "dream" features such as a low profile grille, electrically operated convertible top and windows, no running boards, fender extensions into doors, recessed taillights, and a power hood. Many of these features, considered too innovative or too expensive for production at the time, eventually found their way into passenger cars of the 1950s.

And the Band Played On
In 1940, GM's Waldorf show was supplemented with huge paintings of laborers producing auto components and an operating cutaway demonstrating the elapsed time between the 1941 Oldsmobile's Hydra-Matic transmission shift points. As a preview of things to come, GM added live musical entertainment to their show. *General Motors*

1932 GM Industrialist's Luncheon
In the beginning, the cars were the stars and enhancements were limited to divisional identity panels, a scattering of funeral bouquets, Persian rugs, and a few spotlights. A theme center featuring paintings of outdoor landscapes appears to hold little interest of the attendees, and most of the ladies present appear to be watching from the first floor balcony. *General Motors*

Probably the most famous production design feature inspired by the Y-Job was the bombsight hood ornament. Introduced on the first postwar Buick in 1946, the bombsight carried over until 1948. Some observers were quoted as saying Buick produced bombsights until every kid in the U.S. had one. They became a favorite bicycle accessory, and if you didn't come by one dishonestly you could always go to Western Auto and buy a facsimile for about three bucks. Still available at J.C. Whitney almost fifty years later, the price is up to $17.95.

After the war Mr. Earl had the Y-Job reworked to incorporate wrap-around bumpers and several other minor changes and reintroduced it to the automotive press as a forerunner of postwar design trends. While still unusual compared to early postwar production cars, it soon became outmoded as Mr. Earl's new GM entries began to show forms influenced by military aircraft. This new influence was to be dramatized in the soon-to-appear Motorama Dream Cars.

BELOW
The Advent of Road Shows
This GM all-product show held in San Francisco in 1934 included trucks as well as a full line of passenger cars. GM's non-automotive divisions were recognized with wall banners. *General Motors*

*General Motors Show
San Francisco 1934
Decorations & Lighting by
J L Stuart Mfg Co.*

Who Fathered the Motoramas?

A number of individuals have been credited with having initiated the Motoramas . . . for a number of reasons. Speculation ranges from Alfred P. Sloan to Harlow Curtice and on to Harley Earl, for reasons extending from increasing sales in targeted geographic areas to consumer acceptance of advance styling and engineering features on future cars.

Let's explore some of these possibilities. Alfred Sloan, as president of GM, did begin introducing GM's automotive products at the Waldorf Astoria starting back in 1931. Called "Industrialist's Luncheons" catering to an invitation-only audience of select bankers and Wall Street movers and shakers, these events continued until World War II. The first postwar Waldorf show however, didn't occur until 1949, three years after Mr. Sloan's retirement as chief executive officer.

Harlow Curtice became president of GM in 1953, a position he held until his retirement in 1958. Educated with a business-school background, Curtice was credited with leading Buick Division from the depths of depression to the heights of success. While he had a flair for showmanship, Mr. Curtice was probably too involved in addressing and overseeing GM's most aggressive plant expansion in corporate history to have fathered the Motoramas. During his first four years in office he led GM in investing more than $2.25 billion in new plants and equipment—an effort which hardly left time or energy to devote to show biz.

Harley Earl was the dean of GM styling from 1927 until his retirement as vice-president of GM in 1959. Sometimes referred to as "the father of GM's Motoramas," Mr. Earl, if not more responsible than any other executive for their existence, probably made better use of these extravaganzas than anyone else. Recognizing that a significant segment of the public resisted radical change in fashion as well as styling, he used the Motoramas as an introduction of future ideas, and he carefully observed and listened to audience reaction before incorporating or discarding these concepts in future consumer products.

While these individuals were all prominent in GM's history during the Motorama era of the late 1940s through the early 1960s, GM's sales staff claimed the reason for the Motoramas was to increase overall GM automobile sales through boosting product awareness in selected cities. High-population urban centers such as New York, Los Angeles, San Francisco, and Boston were targeted as locations that needed a jolt to spur added sales. Unfortunately 1958 and 1961, both Motorama show years, were also recession years in the U.S. economy and saw significant drops in domestic car sales. If GM sales execs believed strongly enough in the Motorama concept to convince their board of directors of its positive sales stimulus, there probably would have been a 1962 Motorama. Unfortunately there wasn't a show, but 1962 did bring the best year for dollar sales and earnings in the corporation's history up until that

Fashion Is Foremost
A stylist's sketch for the 1936 Waldorf product presentation depicts stylishly dressed women and rakish car bodies as prominent elements at the show. In reality, the 1936 production cars weren't this streamlined, and the audience was probably not this attractive. *General Motors*

time. These spectacular financial achievements without the aid of the Motorama spectaculars might have, in fact, led to their demise.

My own feeling is that Mr. Sloan, Mr. Curtice, and Mr. Earl, as well as the efforts of GM's sales staff, all were responsible for the Motoramas. As GM's financial watchdogs observed the expense of Mr. Sloan's Industrialist's Luncheons compound, someone probably suggested that if the costs for this event could be amortized over more attendees, the per capita cost would come down. Mr. Curtice might have suggested that the show be opened to the New York public and expanded to four or five days. Sales in the New York city area might have shown an improvement immediately following the first public show in 1949, but it might have taken a second success in 1950 to convince the corporate money men they were onto something. After this second successful event the sales staff might have suggested the show go on tour to see if it could work its magic elsewhere.

So it wasn't until 1953 that the first major Motorama tour was launched, which included a January opening in New York, followed by stops in Miami, Los Angeles, San Francisco, Dallas, and Kansas City. This might have been a little overkill, as the tour concept never again reached six cities in the same year, but it did chart the course for spreading the show cost over more than a million spectators in several population centers.

It was at this 1953 tour that Mr. Earl introduced the Dream Car concept to Motorama audiences . . . in a big way! This was the first public introduction of Cadillac's LeMans, Oldsmobile's Starfire, Pontiac's Bonneville Special and Parisienne, and Buick's Wildcat I.

Rebuilding at the Waldorf
Demonstrating a problem that was to compound in the 1950s is this Cadillac V-16 Fleetwood Convertible Sedan. Too large to fit on the Waldorf's freight elevator, it had to be partially dismantled and ramped to the second floor. This beauty was one of six cars of this model built in 1936 and it was priced at $8,850 in an era when most production cars sold for less than $1,000. *General Motors*

RIGHT
The Best of 1938
The 1938 GM Salon Show at the Waldorf featured two or three production examples from each division, surrounding a central wishing well floral theme center flanked by two Cadillacs and two LaSalles. The dual-side-mounted-rumble-seat LaSalle convertible coupe in the foreground is identical to one currently in the collection of author Bruce Berghoff. His research into this model reveals that approximately thirty survivors remain out of the 819 originally produced V-8-powered art-deco masterpieces. *General Motors*

As if five weren't enough, Mr. Earl added the Buick LeSabre and the XP 300 of 1951 plus the first production Corvette. What a kick-off to what was to become a string of totally conceptual vehicles to be launched before Motorama audiences by the end of the decade!

So it appears many executives and staffs shared in initiating and benefiting from the traveling shows, but maybe it was the challenge of the financial staff more than anything else that was responsible for creating the Motorama phenomenon.

The People Behind the Show

As evidenced by photos of some of GM's pre-World War II Industrialist's Luncheons, decorations at the Waldorf's Grand Ballroom were mostly floral in nature. What started out in the shows of the early 1930s as a scattering of potted plants and funeral parlor-like baskets of ferns, grew into full blown gardens by the late 1930s and early 1940s.

Full-scale, twenty-foot evergreens grew from the balcony, and fresh-cut cedar boughs lined the walls surrounding a theme center of cascading cut flowers or even a miniature wishing well complete with fountain.

Handling these floral extravaganzas was the responsibility of George Wittbold, proprietor of a floral and craft shop located in Chicago. With each passing year, GM's expectations became more and more ambitious, and George, with his competent staff, met the challenge. Toward the last prewar years, George moved his staff to New York and, with the assistance of architects, enhanced the shows with custom planters and modest stage structures. Wall graphics were introduced to begin establishing a theme to the annual product presentations.

Wittbold retired in 1941 and sold his display shop interest to Earl Cappel and Elton MacDonald of Dayton, who enticed Harold B. Stubbs of Detroit to manage their relocated business in Detroit's old Convention Hall.

This group got organized just in time for GM to discontinue all show activities during the war years 1942–45.

Because of GM's inability to meet pent-up consumer demand immediately after the war, management felt product promotion would be an aggravation to an

First of the Dream Cars
Harley Earl used the Y-Job as his personal transportation following its public introduction in 1940. Together, they frequented many of Detroit's exclusive social clubs and entertained the elite with the car's mechanical and electrical innovations. *Buick Public Relations*

already hungry market, but this situation resolved itself by the late 1940s. Competition once again reigned in the market place, and GM was focused on retaining its 50-percent-plus share of market.

The stage was set for GM kicking off its strongest promotion push ever, and what better introduction than another Waldorf showing? But this time it would be opened to the general public, and wives would be invited. Special attractions would have to be designed to appeal to women, and live music would be used to introduce new car offerings to a general audience. To fill this scenario, more than a florist's efforts would be required. Much more!

Into this opportunity stepped Harold B. Stubbs, known as "Cap" from his high school football days. The lean war years cost Cap his business partners; nonetheless, he reorganized as the H. B. Stubbs Company and survived by building war materiel crates for Chrysler. Cap was known as a "heads-up" guy who knew how to spot opportunity and was learning what to do with it. Having had some exposure to prewar GM shows as a young trainee working for Fisher Body, it didn't take Cap long to successfully court Fisher's display business after the war . . . and shortly an industry was born.

Planning for a typical Motorama exhibit program began more than a year before show time. Themes and design concepts were developed by GM Styling's Product and Exhibit Studio, headed by LeRoy Kiefer. Jack Dideon, Kiefer's chief designer, led a group of creative exhibit and graphic designers, including Roger

They Put the Motorama on the Road
Left to right: LeRoy Kiefer, head of the product and exhibit design studio of GM styling; T. H. "Bob" Roberts, show manager of the Motoramas; Spencer D. Hopkins, director of the GM sales section and executive in charge of the Motoramas; and H. B. "Cap" Stubbs, independent contractor in charge of building and installing the shows. *General Motors*

Aten, Don Far, Frank Ramsey, Al Nakota, Don Stuart, Dan Lew, Tom Bradley, Marty Weil, Jim Pascale, Jerry Lockhart, and Fred Overcash in working out every detail from overall showroom decor, vehicle platforms and turntables, audience participation exhibits, and signage down to the graphic design of V.I.P. invitations. Specifications were developed for custom-woven drapery fabrics, colors and finishes, electrical fixtures, and even the flowers and plants used to enhance the atmosphere of the shows.

Where Dreams Were Born
The H. B. Stubbs plant in Warren, Michigan, was where many of the Motoramas were built. The high bay building on the right was designed to duplicate the dimensions of the Waldorf ballroom, allowing pre-assembly of show props and stage mechanisms before transporting to New York. In 1960, an entirely new building was completed just in time to build the 1961 Motorama. Having no inkling that the Motoramas would soon come to an end, Cap Stubbs had a replica of the Waldorf ballroom built into the new plant. *H. B. Stubbs Company*

As designs and specifications were finalized, they were turned over to GM's Bob Smith. His staff prepared detailed architectural and mechanical drawings to facilitate construction. Smith's talented crew included Gordon Gilbert, Fred Braun, Nick Kalopus, Lou Galfant, Ed Graun, Larry Wineman, Frank Trimmer, Al Wigent, Nick Capelli, Paul Powder, and Bob Tuxall, who related this information to Gerry Russello and author Bruce Berghoff at H. B. Stubbs Company.

Stubbs' general shop superintendent, Ludwig Hander, an old-world German cabinet maker, choreographed shop crews consisting of show-skilled cabinet makers, metal workers, upholsterers, plastic workers, electricians, sign writers, and painters. As detailed drawings began arriving, a core crew of about forty men expanded to an army of hundreds. Hander commanded these programs with the authority of a field marshal and demanded a level of exhibit quality consistent with the GM products they would showcase.

He began construction programs by conducting a tape measure check. Every craftsman was required to submit his tape measure or folding rule to be checked against an eight-foot measurement standard. If the tape or rule varied marginally from Hander's standard, it was banished from the shop and had to be replaced with an acceptable substitute.

Every show prop and wall system was engineered to disassemble into pieces that could be packed conveniently into a semi-trailer, and didn't exceed the weight or size capacity of the Waldorf freight elevator. Waldorf ballroom decorative accessories and stage structures were pre-assembled and fit into a special high-bay room attached to the H. B. Stubbs plant that duplicated the dimensions of the Waldorf Grand Ballroom. Here, fits could be checked and modified if necessary to eliminate surprises during the final set-up in New York, where time was of an essence. Following this trial assembly, structures were broken down into their engineered components and fitted into specially built, padded shipping cases. A skilled group of specialists handled this aspect of the packing process, making crates with a coded identity to facilitate truck loading in a precise sequence to conform to the re-assembly schedule at the show site.

As exhibit packing was completed, crates were loaded onto a fleet of uniquely painted Motorama trailers hauled by tractors provided and driven by a distinctly uniformed crews employed by Anchor Motor Freight Incorporated of Michigan. Spectators at the various Motorama locations greeted this fleet with the anticipation of the circus arriving in town.

From a Concert of Talents

Starting with conceptual show sketches, further refined into renderings and then scale models, GM styling's product and exhibit group's final product was a massive set of detailed engineering and construction drawings that were literally hundreds of pages long with written specifications, material samples, and color chips. Finely detailed scale models were designed and constructed under LeRoy Kiefer's directions, which were initially used to study the three-dimensional feeling of the show. After finalizing, they were used to sell GM's marketing group the sizzle of the show's concept. Ultimately, pieces of the model were used to supplement detailed drawings delivered to H. B. Stubbs Company, to further inform the construction process. Sometimes, these models became sets for the GM photo-graphic staff's motion picture magic, and a "sell" film was produced to assist in influencing the corporate money men. Mr. Kiefer consistently encouraged his creative group to disregard reality and shoot for the moon. Once, I made the mistake of challenging some of his specifications as being unnecessarily extravagant. Seems as how a large number of display panels had been detailed to be four feet, six inches wide rather than the standard plywood and Masonite dimension of four feet wide. I think I said some-thing like, "If God had wanted plywood to be four feet, six inches wide he would have grown trees that size." I think Mr. Kiefer's response was, "If God had wanted you to be a designer, he would have put you to work on my staff!"
General Motors

CHAPTER 2

1949: Transportation Unlimited

General Motors staged its first postwar auto show in January 1949. Headlined "Transportation Unlimited" it was GM's first all corporate sponsored show at New York's Waldorf Astoria, which was opened to the public.

Laid out on the ballroom floor between the "wheel" and the "column" were two production vehicles each by Chevrolet, Pontiac, Oldsmobile, Buick, and Cadillac. Sixteen additional production cars were exhibited in rooms adjacent to the ballroom. Also featured were audience participation engineering and research displays to preview some of GM's technical thinking for the future.

Minuscule in size by today's auto-show standards, the show was a great success, drawing over 300,000 public attendees in its eight-day run. Following its New York stand, Transportation Unlimited moved to Detroit for an additional eight-day run in mid-April and again drew almost 300,000 spectators when staged in Detroit's old Convention Hall.

Total cost of the two-city show came to $1,630,000, which in those days was a significant merchandising budget. Prorated between the five car divisions on a "fifty-fifty" basis, each division split the first 50 percent equally and the second 50 percent on the basis of their consumer influence appropriations. Other participating divisions were charged a nominal amount on a flat-rate basis. Costs of the prewar Waldorf shows had simply been split equally between the five car divisions.

While GM's special styling vehicles and Dream Cars would not appear at public shows for another four years, GM's car divisions each had their own batch of surprises for show audiences.

Buick displayed its newly bodied Riviera featuring the first modern hardtop offered on a U.S.-built production car. A less significant innovation was Buick's

Emphasizing Details
In addition to venti-port perforated fender trim, Buick capitalized on the popularity of their bombsight hood ornament, introduced on the 1938 Y-Job and 1946 production models, with this giant handrail decoration. *General Motors*

Farewell to Arms
A stage show featuring a cast of some twenty actors and actresses backed by a name band performed six thirty-minute shows daily in a series of pantomime skits which combined the presentation of GM's production cars with the very latest in the field of fashion. On the custom, raised turntable stage, the "Wheel of Fashion," one car from each of the five automotive divisions emerged in sequence, made two revolutions on the "wheel," and exited behind the stage in the left wing. *General Motors*

venti-port perforated fender that, to the chagrin of Buick's management, made a more lasting impression on the market than Buick's hardtop introduction.

Chevrolet introduced its all new slab-side body design in both the fastback and bustle-back roof configurations. Consumer acceptance of these models was reflected in a calendar-year production of more than 1.1 million units, which established an all-time Chevrolet production record to date.

Pontiac featured a Chieftan DeLuxe Eight coupe sedan with whitewalls and fender skirts. Contributing to reaching a production total of 3 million units built since 1926 were two new Pontiac car lines, a notch-backed A-body model newly named the Chieftan and a fastbacked B-body named the Streamliner. Pontiac also introduced its first domestic truck since the 1920s in the form of a station-wagon-based sedan delivery.

Oldsmobile offered its Holiday Coupe version of its "A"-bodied hardtop which helped them achieve a 56 percent sales increase over calendar year 1948, and the highest sales level since its founding in 1897.

Cadillac took the lead amongst its sister divisions in using the corporate shows to reveal specially modified show cars. At this 1949 extravaganza, four of Cadillac's seven car offerings were customized. Starting with a Coupe DeVille pillarless two-door hardtop, Cadillac followed with two modified Fleetwood Sixty Specials and a Series 62 Convertible styled with a western interior.

Thus began the tradition of revealing futuristic ideas to public audiences to measure their reactions to innovation.

Art from Art

I frequently marveled at the mix of unusual talents that the exhibit industry attracted and ultimately made productive. During the Motorama era there were no display trade schools or colleges offering courses in exhibit design or management. The industry took a strange assortment of individuals and, if successful, choreographed their efforts into producing effective story telling-devices and three-dimensional demonstrations.

One of the most talented individuals at H. B. Stubbs Company was a displaced fine artist by the name of Art Serth. Art's passion was oil painting and his specialty was skies and landscapes. He could create depth on canvas so convincingly you could walk into his paintings. Art merged his painting technique with an acquired skill for model making and became the in-house Diorama Department.

An old time favorite of Art's is the ever-popular animated diorama "American Crossroads." Crossroads tells the story of the industrialization of middle America over a fifty-year period. Starting with scenes of untouched timber and grazing lands, slowly converting to village settlements and finally to contemporary cities, the story is told through the voice of a clever narration as three-sided surface panels flip to reveal new scenery. Measuring almost twenty feet wide by eight feet deep, this diorama was originally built in the mid-1940s for GM's Parade of Progress and after traveling hundreds of thousands of miles, was briefly retired to a display room in the Detroit GM building in the 1970s.

The newly revived American Crossroads is now on display in the GM Motorama permanent exhibit at Chicago's Museum of Science and Industry.

Over forty-five years of informing and entertaining American family audiences . . . a true tribute to Art Serth!

Jimmy Wants You

The story of David and Goliath repeated itself often during the hectic days and nights of Motorama labor disputes.

Gerry Russello, small in physical stature but an excellent bargainer when he represented H.B. Stubbs Company in the best interests of General Motors, recalls some thrilling (chilling) events.

One year during the Waldorf show installation, a controversy developed between the laborers and teamsters. Laborers had traditionally moved display materials from the hotel loading dock to the second floor Grand Ballroom, ready to be unpacked and assembled by carpenters or millwrights.

The teamsters had been on the move to conquer more work at the show-place and decided the Motorama would be an ideal place to stake their claim. A teamster

Postwar Power
At the opposite end of the Waldorf Grand Ballroom, GM erected a twenty-six-foot tower called the "Column of Stars," a five-sided pylon capped with a heroic revolving globe.

Mounted on the five-pointed-star base were the engines of the five GM car lines. *General Motors*

business agent was dispatched to the Waldorf to find Cap Stubbs to explain the new program. As Russello recalls the situation, Cap suddenly disappeared. The business agent was then steered to Russello, and probably thought he was going to be a pushover.

He approached Russello with his well-rehearsed opener, "Jimmy Hoffa wants to see you!" Unimpressed by this request, Russello responded, "If Hoffa wants to see me he's going to have to come here, 'cause I can't leave the job site."

Russello didn't hold his breath and Jimmy didn't visit the Motorama, but a compromise was reached before the next shift reported for work.

Another memorable negotiation took place in Boston, when a dispute arose regarding the cleaning of exhibits and polishing of show cars. Russello was asked to contact the business agent of one of the unions involved. Invited to meet the agent at Boston's well-known Dinty Moore's restaurant, Russello thought nothing unusual of the invitation until he discovered the deli was located in a downtown alley. Undaunted, Russello kept the appointment but had second thoughts when the business agent lit up a big cigar, pulled back his suit coat, and revealed a shoulder holster complete with hardware.

Russello seems to have forgotten the outcome of that meeting, but the show went on!

A Gathering of Mouse Holes

While the major innovation shown at the Buick display was the all new Riviera featuring the first modern hardtop body design, the element that caused the most publicity was the new venti-ports on the front fenders. Referred to by some as "mouseholes," they had negligible functional purpose, but remained as a Buick exclusive for more than twenty years. *General Motors*

Western Special
One of 8,000 series 62 Cadillac convertible coupes built for
the 1949 model year. This one-off special featured calfskin
carpets. *General Motors*

CHAPTER 3

1950: Midcentury Motorama

For the first time, GM applied the name "Motorama" to a traveling public show. Previously "Motorama" was adopted to name GM's permanent exhibit at Chicago's Museum of Science and Industry, which opened in 1947 to present GM's story of "Fifty Years of Automotive Progress" to a mostly student audience.

The Midcentury Motorama opened a nine-day run at the Waldorf on January 19, 1950. Again, actors and music were blended to present the first half century in five skits on a custom-built, revolving stage.

The show again utilized the five rooms flanking the ballroom, and this time dedicated one room to each of the five divisions, allowing for the display of twenty-two additional cars.

Most of the technical exhibits introduced in the 1949 show were deleted, and an Allison turbo-prop aircraft engine display was added.

Frigidaire kitchen appliances were shown downstairs on the hotel mezzanine, and Chevrolet and GMC truck pictorial displays were added on the first balcony.

New York attendance went up to 320,580 spectators, and costs were slightly below one million for the one-city show tour for 1950.

Fooled Once . . . Shame on Us!

When we came into most Motorama towns, we were usually greeted as the "big shooters" from "Big D" . Detroit. In other than an occasional union skirmish, GM

Wheel of Fortune
At the ballroom center was a huge "cloverleaf" five-car turntable and tower featuring the various car lines. Nine additional production cars were positioned around the ballroom. *General Motors*

Building the Wheel
The public had little appreciation of the complex machinery and thousands of man hours required to assemble and decorate the sub-structure of the five-car turntable. *General Motors*

brass and our H. B. Stubbs crew pretty much had things their way. Convention-facility managers and local politicians and contractors rolled over and played dead if necessary to maintain repeat visits. But I sensed the Waldorf attitude was different.

It might have had something to do with the feeling that only the blacksmith end of the auto business was conducted in Detroit . . . while the life blood of that industry, money management, was reserved for New York. Whatever it was, it was obvious that the Waldorf management ran a business, and ran it damn well.

Case in point: Every year that the big show visited the Waldorf, numerous scrapes and dents would be inflicted on the grand old lady's walls, columns, and sometimes ceilings.

After all, she wasn't designed for mega-ton car platforms and turntables, and we somewhat doubted that her architects ever envisioned even one automobile darkening the ballroom floor.

Well, one year after our New York tour we were told that GM's show management received an invoice from the Waldorf, rumored to be in the six figures range, to cover repair costs to the building. Undoubtedly the damage reported was an accumulation of assaults from who knows how many temporary tenants over how many years. Regardless, we heard GM had little defense, so it probably settled in order to pave its way back to the Waldorf in future years.

General Motors might have been burned once, but was not about to let it happen twice. Those blacksmiths from "Big D" knew a thing or two about street fighting. Prior to occupying the Waldorf for the next show, GM dispatched a crew of architects and photographers to New York to visually and verbally document every chip, scratch and mar, not only in the showrooms but inside freight elevators, storage rooms and below-scenes tunnels. I understand the repair bill shrank significantly that year.

18

Springboard to the Top

Having joined GM's styling group as a novice designer in 1949, Chuck Jordan was given mostly non-automotive assignments working with truck and train design. Chuck's contributions to the Aerotrain, the Cameo Carrier, and GMC's L'Universelle Dream Truck prompted his boss, Bill Mitchell, to say, "If you're going to get anywhere around here you have to get involved with passenger cars." This provocation led to Chuck designing what was to become the Buick Centurion, unveiled in 1956.

He recalls that Mr. Earl and Mr. Mitchell defined the Dream Car design objectives for each division in a very general way, leaving the specifics up to each designer. Typically an assignment might be outlined as boldly as, "We need a hot four-door for Buick" or "Let's create LaSalle as a small car in a time frame when production cars are big."

Chuck, retired in 1992 as GM's vice president of design, says the beauty of the Dream Car exercises in future concepts was management's philosophy of, "Let the cat out of the bag and really go for it!" . . . and the results of that philosophy comes through in many of the Dream Cars.

Danish Interpretation

Hundreds of sheets of drawings were prepared by General Motors styling's product and exhibit group for every show. Details frequently were complete, down to the exact location of screws and fasteners which would eventually be concealed by paint finishes or upholstery. As in any undertaking of this immensity, occasionally things got screwed up.

One incident that comes to mind involved a prospective sub-contractor, Hans B. Nielsen, art metalsmith extrordinaire. Nielsen introduced himself to us with a very well written letter enumerating his vast design, engineering, and prototype construction experience in Denmark, having worked on projects for some of Scandinavia's leading architects and furniture designers of the 1940s. His resume read like the answer to an exhibit builder's wildest dream. This guy could do anything, or so it seemed from the letter, which we found out later was written by one of Nielsen's customers who wanted him to succeed in America regardless of his past experience.

After being summoned by phone, Nielsen arrived wearing Danish wooden soled shoes and a fresh off-the-boat accent. As I walked him through several drawings detailing custom brass appliance handles to be used in Frigidaire's Kitchen of Tomorrow exhibit, Nielsen nodded his understanding at every page. As a starter assignment, I

The Cadillac Debutante

A forerunner of the Dream Cars, this specially trimmed and gold painted Series 62 convertible featured an interior upholstered with 187 Somali leopard pelts and hardware plated in sixteen-carat gold. Valued at the then fantastic sum of $30,000, this car was allegedly the inspiration for the Hollywood movie The *Solid Gold Cadillac*. Shown behind the wheel is Mrs. Ivan S. Ingels, daughter of former GM chairman Albert Bradley. Imagine the reaction this specialty vehicle would get from today's environmentalists. *General Motors*

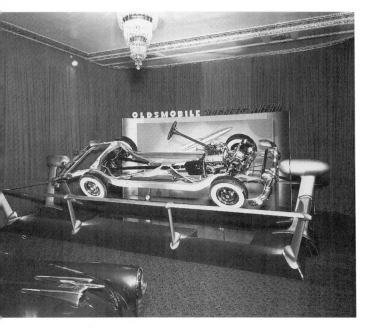

Ready For Action
Oldsmobile featured their Rocket engine in this stripped-down, glamorous, chassis display. *General Motors*

gave him two sets of hardware to complete in the next two weeks, and he departed promising perfection.

About two days later he arrived carrying the finished product, and the handles looked like golden jewelry. As he unwrapped each piece he waited for my approval, and described every step of their fabrication. When they were all spread out Nielsen beamed with pride, and I looked more carefully at the group. Something prompted me to pull out the drawings and when I compared the parts I was speechless. Each piece had been sculpted exactly backward from the drawings. Sensing my concern, Nielsen asked if there was a problem. When I explained the discrepancy he asked if the drawings I had provided weren't European projection. Not being familiar with this term I proceeded to make a perspective sketch of one of the parts the way it should look. "Ooh, dat's English projection—no problem!"

I still felt badly a couple of days later when Nielsen returned with the corrected pieces.

From this rocky beginning we developed a business relationship which lasted thirty-five years. Nielsen finally retired for the third time at age seventy-six when he sold his tools and machinery.

How to find your way around GM's MIDCENTURY MOTORAMA

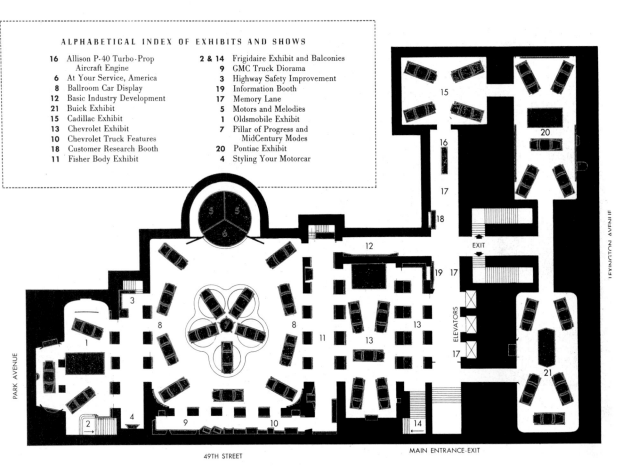

ALPHABETICAL INDEX OF EXHIBITS AND SHOWS

16 Allison P-40 Turbo-Prop Aircraft Engine	2 & 14 Frigidaire Exhibit and Balconies
6 At Your Service, America	9 GMC Truck Diorama
8 Ballroom Car Display	3 Highway Safety Improvement
12 Basic Industry Development	19 Information Booth
21 Buick Exhibit	17 Memory Lane
15 Cadillac Exhibit	5 Motors and Melodies
13 Chevrolet Exhibit	1 Oldsmobile Exhibit
10 Chevrolet Truck Features	7 Pillar of Progress and MidCentury Modes
18 Customer Research Booth	20 Pontiac Exhibit
11 Fisher Body Exhibit	4 Styling Your Motorcar

Mid-century Motorama Program
The Waldorf show was so spread out that GM provided spectators with a floor plan. *General Motors*

CHAPTER 4

1953: Motorythms and Fashion Firsts

Not having experienced a Motorama for two years, New York was ready in January of 1953. The industry was also ready for a long-needed sales jolt. General Motors' domestic car and truck sales had tumbled from an all-time high to date of over 3.5 million units in 1950 to 2.25 million units two years later. Prompted by this 30 percent decline, GM was ready for some hard selling. In what was to become the longest tour in the history of the Motoramas, the show opened at the Waldorf, followed by stops in Miami, Los Angeles, San Francisco, Dallas, and a close in Kansas City. Six months of touring to an audience of almost 1.5 million spectators, and GM didn't spare the horses. They spent over $5 million on shows and exhibits over and above the cost of producing seven Dream Cars to wow this huge audience. In comparison to the average $250,000 cost of a typical Broadway stage show at that time, GM was probably the biggest single entertainment investor in the world.

"Motorythms and Fashion Firsts" became the stage show theme. Richard and Edith Barstow of Barnum & Bailey Circus fame were retained by the Kudner Agency to choreograph and produce a seven-car stage spectacular highlighted by the LeSabre and XP-300 Dream Cars.

Hanging the Ceiling

One of the first steps in preparing the Waldorf Hotel ballroom in New York for the Motorama show was to "hang the ceiling." This really meant unpacking a number of dark blue velvet fabric panels and tacking one edge to a special strip that

Outdrew Washington
From 11:30 A.M. to 1:00 P.M. on January 23, 1953, over 12,000 visitors passed through the Motorama show at the Waldorf, totally ignoring the swearing into office of President Dwight Eisenhower. *General Motors*

had been secured all the way around the ballroom above the second balcony. When all of the panels were tacked, they were joined at room center and hoisted up about fifty feet high to create a "festoon" effect and completely obscure the ornate plaster ceiling. After all, GM wanted the audience to look at its products, not admire the turn-of-the-century architecture.

When completely assembled, this fabric ceiling used almost 5,000 yards of velvet weighing over two tons, and required tens of thousands of upholstery tacks to hold it up. If the tacks were to let go during the show, the crowd induced panic would be catastrophic for GM. Charged with this no small responsibility of hanging the ceiling was a local New York decorating contractor, Frank W. Stevens Company and it's experienced foreman Carl Droge.

Carl was an old German with a heart of gold and many tales of learning the trade of "tack spitting" the hard way. If you ever read the word "sterilized" on a box of upholstery tacks, that would be your first clue about "tack spitting." Old time upholsterers would take a handful of tacks, put them in their mouth, and one at a time with a clever move of the tongue, deliver a tack to their lips with the tack head facing out so it could be picked up by the magnetic end of their tack hammer. This was a danger-

Taking a Flyer
This lovely damsel is about to be launched into the Waldorf balcony. *General Motors*

XP-300 Buick
One of the most famous Dream Cars of all time, the XP-300 was actually unveiled to the public in 1951 but held over for the 1953 Motorama because of sustained public interest.

Here it's driven by Charles Chayne, who supervised its development at Buick, and admired by Ivan Wiles, Buick's general manager. *General Motors*

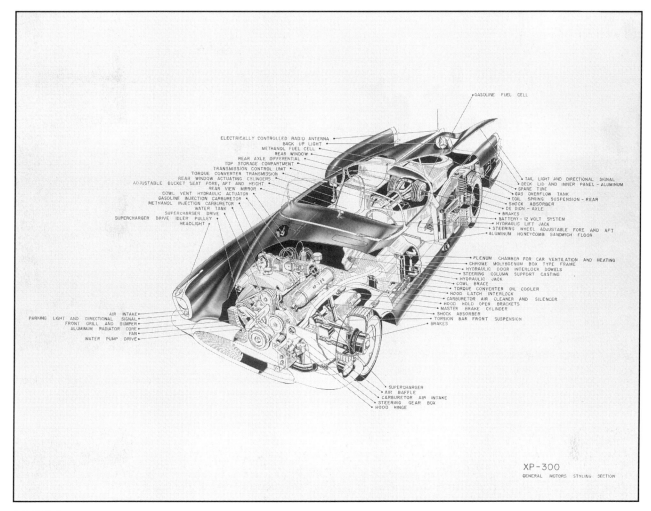

XP-300 Cutaway
Powered by a supercharged 215-cubic-inch V-8 engine delivering 335 horsepower, the XP-300 ran on a mixture of gasoline and methanol delivered from two separate tanks. *General Motors*

ous skill at best, and not one to be undertaken when you had the hiccups, or even a mild cold.

Carl was the best when it came to tack spitting, having learned his trade during prohibition. While most of his contemporaries went hungry, Carl found an opportunity to work by hanging drapes on the walls of basement dungeons around Manhattan. His employers paid cash and gave him all the "pop" he wanted to drink after he finished the job. As the speak-easy industry flourished, so did Carl, but it almost came to a sudden end one morning. Seems Carl had been burning the candle at both ends, and one night after putting in a long two days shift, he accidentally fell asleep in the loft of a speak-easy. He was awakened the next morning when he overheard the proprietors discussing a "hit" on the floor below him. Carl learned the art of complete silence that day.

In spite of the numerous hazards of climbing the ceiling and walls of the Waldorf, Carl felt safer working with GM than his earlier clients.

Dreams Come True

The Dinner Key Exposition Building located on the waterfront in south Miami was built originally as a huge steel complex to house Pan-American clipper ships. After the growth of the commercial aircraft industry led to primarily land-based planes, the Dinner Key complex was eventually converted to a public convention facility, owned by the City of Miami.

Buddy Clewis, a good ol' boy from Louisiana (or thereabouts) was the Dinner Key building manager during most of the GM Motorama shows that came to Miami. Buddy appeared pretty laid back, even comatose at times, but he had a network of friends that were ready, able, and willing to provide for, or arrange to provide for, any and all the needs that installing a GM Motorama in Miami required. He also had a knack for clearing January and sometimes even December bookings from the calendar so that GM would get first crack at the choice winter dates whenever they wanted them. Sometimes on the municipal events calendar, shows would be announced that were figments of Buddy's imagination, conceived to provide GM with time for a more leisurely installation schedule. No one worked harder to welcome GM or accommodate its needs.

Buddy, in addition to being a "host extraordinaire," had a penchant for impressive cars. Fire-engine-red Buick Roadmaster convertibles with all the goodies would be just fine . . . and, as luck would have it, GM built such cars. Buddy said he never knew how it happened, but after every Motorama show in Miami he found a new Buick convert parked in his driveway, all gassed and ready to go.

Ring for Room Service

Back when GM enjoyed over 50 percent sales penetration of the U.S. market, executive perks ran ram-

OPPOSITE LOWER
Spinning the Duke
Behind the wheel of his favorite LeSabre, Harley Earl takes the Duke for a spin. The Duke of Windsor, a resident of the Waldorf for many years, was a frequent guest as well as sidewalk superintendent at the Motoramas. Notice the long knot in the Duke's tie, perhaps the origination of the "Windsor" knot? *General Motors*

BELOW
LeSabre Cutaway
Featuring extensive use of aluminum and magnesium, this rolling laboratory weighed in at less than 3,000 pounds. Among its innovations was a rain-activated electric top. *General Motors*

Buick LeSabre
Perhaps because the ladies loved it, or maybe because of its styling and mechanical innovations, this aircraft-inspired car became Harley Earl's personal ride for several years. *General Motors*

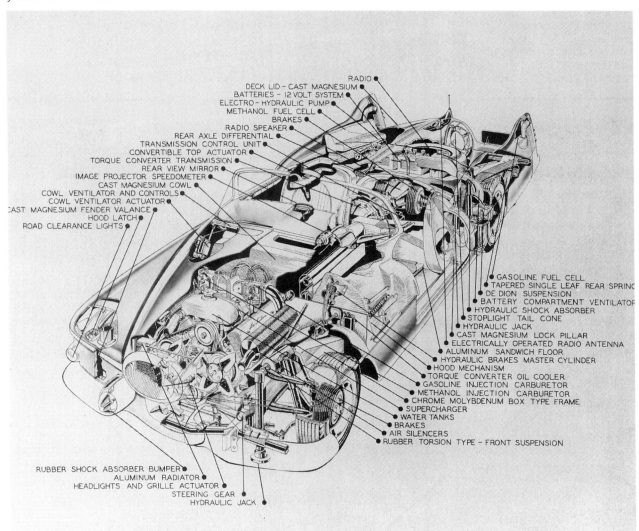

RADIO
DECK LID – CAST MAGNESIUM
BATTERIES – 12 VOLT SYSTEM
ELECTRO – HYDRAULIC PUMP
METHANOL FUEL CELL
BRAKES
RADIO SPEAKER
REAR AXLE DIFFERENTIAL
TRANSMISSION CONTROL UNIT
CONVERTIBLE TOP ACTUATOR
TORQUE CONVERTER TRANSMISSION
REAR VIEW MIRROR
IMAGE PROJECTOR SPEEDOMETER
CAST MAGNESIUM COWL
COWL VENTILATOR AND CONTROLS
COWL VENTILATOR ACTUATOR
CAST MAGNESIUM FENDER VALANCE
HOOD LATCH
ROAD CLEARANCE LIGHTS

GASOLINE FUEL CELL
TAPERED SINGLE LEAF REAR SPRING
DE DION SUSPENSION
BATTERY COMPARTMENT VENTILATOR
HYDRAULIC SHOCK ABSORBER
STOPLIGHT TAIL CONE
HYDRAULIC JACK
CAST MAGNESIUM LOCK PILLAR
ELECTRICALLY OPERATED RADIO ANTENNA
ALUMINUM SANDWICH FLOOR
HYDRAULIC BRAKES MASTER CYLINDER
HOOD MECHANISM
TORQUE CONVERTER OIL COOLER
GASOLINE INJECTION CARBURETOR
METHANOL INJECTION CARBURETOR
CHROME MOLYBDENUM BOX TYPE FRAME
SUPERCHARGER
WATER TANKS
BRAKES
AIR SILENCERS
RUBBER TORSION TYPE – FRONT SUSPENSION

RUBBER SHOCK ABSORBER BUMPER
ALUMINUM RADIATOR
HEADLIGHTS AND GRILLE ACTUATOR
STEERING GEAR
HYDRAULIC JACK

THE DREAM CAR CULT
Sweating the Details—Tony Ciminera,
Haworth, New Jersey

From a kid born in Brooklyn in 1939 who went on to have an automotive career spanning Studebaker-Packard, *Motor Trend* magazine, Fiat of North America, *Road & Track*, stints with Malcolm Bricklin, and now as an industry consultant comes the statement, "Its been great fun, and it all started with the Motoramas."

Ciminera admits he was first turned-on to cars when his dad came home with a brand new 1951 Buick Super—the first new car purchased by his family since Tony was born—but it was his attending the New York Motorama that turned up the heat on his auto enthusiasm.

He vividly recalls his teenage train and bus ride from New Jersey to Manhattan, waiting his turn in long lines on 49th Street in cold winter weather, and finally getting in to see the Motorama. And it was all worth it.

Here was Ciminera's first time to see a true one-off car built by a major corporation in a first class way: "Built the way a car should be built . . . demon-

strating what America was capable of doing. Let your imagination run wild, and America could build it! But GM didn't just build sexy cars—they sweated the details."

Ciminera remembers the custom-designed GM styling medallion mounted low on the fenders of the Dream Cars. "No other American manufacturer would think about doing that, and that same attention to detail carried over into GM's production cars."

Ciminera's obsession with detail has nurtured a fondness for scale-model cars, trucks, and busses. Over 600 of them now grace the glass shelves of his custom designed and built showcases. During his search for model cars, he has also acquired a vast collection of automotive and Motorama literature.

Ciminera dreams of someday doing an auto show limited to dream and prototype models and wistfully says, "God, I wish the Motorama was back!"

Tony Ciminera
T. Ciminera

ABOVE
Cadillac Orleans
Featuring suicide doors, the Orleans introduced the four-door hardtop concept, which appeared in production three years later. *General Motors*

OPPOSITE TOP
Buick Wildcat I
One of GM's first all-fiberglass prototype bodies, the Buick Wildcat I was used in developing production techniques for the 1953 Corvette. *General Motors*

OPPOSITE LOWER
Pontiac Parisienne
One of the most outstanding Dream Cars for 1953, it contrasted a jet-black exterior with pink leather seats and roof lining. To provide easy access, the front seats automatically moved back twelve inches when the doors were opened. *General Motors*

pant. Rarely did vice-presidents or divisional general managers travel out of Detroit without an entourage of assistants hovering to take care of their every wish.

Prior to one year's Motorama west coast tour, one of these assistants discovered that his boss's favorite soft drink was not marketed in California. Stepping in to save the day, the assistant rushed over to the loading area of the show trucks with a delivery of five or six cases of the boss's brew. Since the cargo wasn't foremost in the driver's mind, he followed the route plan taking him through the northern states without question. When the trailer was opened in Los Angeles, the floor was a sea of foam, resulting from six cases of frozen pop spilling their contents everywhere.

Upon discovering the disaster, the executive assistant did what was expected of him . . . he called Detroit and had a GM plane dispatched with six replacement cases.

Another executive who enjoyed a cocktail now and then found "nipping" especially satisfying while cruising from appointment to appointment aboard commercial airlines. Upon being promoted to general manager of his division, a corporate plane was made available to him, which on the surface appeared to be nice perk. Unfortunately, GM rules forbade alcoholic beverages aboard corporate planes. No problem. With a show of executive creativity, the newly appointed vice-president ordered a nice portable liquor case constructed. Finished in gloss white with a bold red cross painted on both sides, no one questioned the arrival of his "first aid kit" before each flight.

Cadillac Le Mans
Styled as a two-seat "sports prototype" and driven by former Cadillac general manager Don Ahrens with Cadillac sales manager James Roche standing by, the lightweight Le Mans predicted the grille and front end used on 1954 Cadillacs. *General Motors*

Olds Starfire
Drawing inspiration from the Lockheed fighter plane of the same name, the X-P Rocket Oldsmobile was intended for four passengers (but not all in the front seat). *General Motors*

Prototype Corvette
First unveiled at the 1953 New York show, this Motorama Corvette underwent some subtle changes before it reached production later in the year. The most obvious differences were the front-fender air scoops, exterior door push buttons, nose-mounted crossed American flag emblem over "Corvette" script, and the downward wing on the front fenders. *General Motors*

Hanging the Ceiling
Thousands of pounds of fabric were held in place with tiny upholstery tacks. *General Motors*

Master of Illusion
Diorama artist Art Serth demonstrates his steady brush. *H. B. Stubbs Company*

Dreams Come True
The Dinner Key Auditorium complex in Miami hosted the
Motorama for four tours. *General Motors*

CHAPTER 5

1954: Going Places

Nineteen fifty-four saw a four-city tour following the traditional New York opening in late January. Miami, Los Angeles, San Francisco, and for a Motorama first, the show went to Chicago in late April to play to standing-room-only audiences. (Actually, all shows played to standing-room-only audiences as there were no seats provided anywhere on the tour.) Attendance reached a show-to-date high of 1,926,864 and cost of the shows also reached a high of $6,239,400.

The stage show "Going Places" was again produced and choreographed by Richard and Edith Barstow. Original music by Vincent Travis played to the presentation of five production cars, one representing each car division on a single-level stage.

A spectacular group of ten Dream Cars surrounded the ever-exciting "cloverleaf" turntable presentation of a representative production convertible from each division.

Don't Fool with Mother Nature

Pappy Blair was a master colorist and paint mixer at H. B. Stubbs. Working with a basic palette of two dozen finely ground lacquer-tinting colors, Blair could match about any color the GM designers could dream up, in flat or semi-gloss finishes. Exotics like metallics and pearlescents, requiring the addition of shiny metal particles or ground fish scales, posed little problem, but every once in a while one of Blair's paint matches would be challenged, usually by a new staff member from GM's design group who hadn't yet grown to respect Blair's expertise.

On one such occasion, a novice advised Blair that his mix required slight adjustment to match the paper color chip that the designer had supplied. After repeating

Cadillac El Camino
This silver-gray fiberglass coupe had a burnished aluminum top. Powered by a 230-horsepower Cadillac engine, the El Camino reached an overall length of 200.6 inches and a height of 51.5 inches. Distinctive rearward-canted fins, hooded quad headlights, and a twin-torpedo front bumper made this easily recognizable as a Cadillac. *General Motors*

More Dreams Than Ever Before
The 1954 Motorama featured ten all-new dream cars.
General Motors

the exercise several times without scoring a bull's-eye, Blair thought he would solve the problem by repainting the designer's color chip with Blair's last mix. In the next review session, presented with four or five variations of the target color plus the ringer that Blair had created, the unsuspecting designer by-passed the ringer and selected the wrong sample as the closest match.

Blair's broad smile was not because a decision was made, but how it was made.

Missing Silverware

Many of the GM engineering and research exhibits featured way-out, science-fiction-like hardware devices. Most of these demonstrations were educational and sometimes even exciting to see, but completely useless if you wanted to take some parts home.

Experimental car radios on the other hand had some practical value, and Delco Radio frequently displayed and demonstrated future concepts in tuning selection and sound at the Motorama shows. Knowing the potential enticement of these sets, we took added precautions to secure the radio chassis and speakers into display cabinets to make them all but theft-proof . . . or so we thought.

Following each show we would repack each exhibit into large, custom-fitted wooden cases, numbered for identification and internally padded for protection. Opening and closing these cases was a time-consuming task, as the removable lids or sides were held on with endless combinations of carriage bolts and wing nuts. I often wondered who ever came up with that system, but never could find anyone who had a clue, other than it had always been done that way. And it wasn't all bad because it gave us something to assign to the slowest, largest, or even the smartest guy in the crew . . . and every crew had at least one that measured up.

One year when we received and unpacked the radio display following a Waldorf showing we discovered sev-

ABOVE
Cadillac La Espada
This sports convertible was mechanically the same as the El Camino coupe, and also was bodied in fiberglass but finished in Apollo Gold. Featuring a specially engineered convertible top with ribbed elements, it created a perfectly curved surface when raised. *General Motors*

eral prototype radios missing, and the obvious attempt to dislodge a couple more. Someone had spent a lot of time working with the correct tools to make such a clean sweep. We also wondered why remains of a lunch, some cigarettes, and an empty pop bottle had been left in the crate. Ultimately, we deduced that this success was the result of teamwork. Someone was probably

OPPOSITE
Firebird XP-21—A Traffic Stopper
Leading the Dream Cars was the Firebird XP-21, probably the most unique and functional of the experimental cars on display. Styled after the Douglas Skyray supersonic jet, the Firebird, usually referred to as Firebird I, was the first U.S.-built car to be powered by a two-section gas-turbine engine. The gasifier section provided a source of compressed hot gas, the energy from which was delivered to the power section of the turbine to the rear wheels. The gasifier actually replaced the engine and torque converter pump in a conventional car, while the power section replaced the torque converter turbine, transmission, and rear-axle gears. Developing 370 horsepower at 26,000 gasifier-turbine rpm and 13,000 power-turbine rpm, this became another Harley Earl legend. *General Motors*

THE DREAM CAR CULT
From Early Memories to Fine Lines—
Bob Eng, Torrance, California

Bob Eng recalls his first Motorama visit at the Pan Pacific Auditorium in Los Angeles in 1954: "I was only thirteen years old and had never seen a live stage show before. That impressed me more than any car-related show has impressed me since."

Eng attended the 1955 show and left with vivid memories: "The Dream Cars were spectacular, especially the 1955 LaSalles and the Biscayne four-door sedan . . . I have been waiting for GM to produce these cars ever since."

Not only was Eng impressed by the staging and Dream Cars, but he sought out every piece of literature, postcard, and souvenir coin he could find. Adding to his collection from the first two shows, Eng visited the final 1961 Motorama and built his file of memorabilia to include more than fifty-eight pieces, and he still has them all today.

As Eng matured, his work took him into computer graphics, and he eventually merged his vocational skills with his hobby. He began creating computer-generated line drawings of GM production cars. This grew to include one or two Dream Cars, and that grew to include every Motorama Dream Car.

To date, Eng has produced over 150 car images on his mighty Macintosh console, and has gravitated into rear views to supplement front three-quarters and profiles as new research photos and literature turn up.

His early Motorama memories have truly generated fine, fine lines!

Bob Eng
K. Berghoff

Cadillac Park Avenue

The Park Avenue, one of two four-door sedan Dream Cars shown in 1954. Powered with a 238 horsepower Cadillac V-8 engine, it carried a 230.1 inch body length, an 80-inch width, and a 58.3-inch height mounted on a production 1954 Cadillac 60 Special chassis. Forward-slanting rear fender fins carried three jet taillights on each side. *General Motors*

OPPOSITE LOWER
Oldsmobile Experimental Cutlass
Named after the U.S. Navy jet, this two-seat sports-model hard-top coupe featured tear-drop stainless steel front wheel openings with engine heat vents, power by the 250-horsepower Rocket V-8 engine with 9:1 compression ratio, and a distinctive rear window with venetian blind shades. *General Motors*

ABOVE
Buick Wildcat II
This sports car was the successor to the 1953 Wildcat I. Built on a 100-inch wheel base and powered by Buick's 220-horsepower V-8 engine, the 170.9-inch fiberglass body reached only 40.2 inches high with the top up. Originally painted Electric Blue, this model still exists, refinished in a metallic platinum. *General Motors*

sealed-up in the crate upstairs in the Waldorf, complete with tools, a flashlight, and lunch. He worked in these cramped quarters until the crate went on the freight elevator, where he and the radios were probably liberated. He didn't quite finish the job, but GM would be back next year with some fresh radios.

While some crates came up with items missing, just as often we would find crates with items added. The most popular treasure to be found after a Waldorf show would be silver-plated tableware, coffee and cream pitchers, and even hotel trays . . . everything

nicely wrapped in hotel tablecloths and towels, and bearing a nice big initial "W."

I suppose we could have checked the crew roster for last names beginning with "W," but I recall collecting all of the "W" stuff, packing it up, and shipping it back to the Waldorf.

NEXT PAGES
Olds F-88
Powered by the same engine as the Cutlass and also a two-seater, this car sported a completely concealed convertible top within its fiberglass body. *General Motors*

Pontiac Strato Streak
A four-door pillarless hardtop sedan was described as a "spectator sports car." Built on a production Star Chief chassis, the Strato Streak featured bucket seats front and rear,

with the front seat mounted on swivels to provide easier entry. *General Motors*

LEFT
Pontiac Bonneville Special
Primarily an experimental competition-type car, the Bonneville Special's clear bubble top featured gull-wing windows. Its wheel base was 100 inches, and it was powered by a straight-eight engine with four two-barrel carbs and a Hydra-Matic transmission. *General Motors*

Chevrolet Corvair
Built on the Corvette chassis with a closed "fastback" coupe design, this car provided ventilation to the passenger area through screened vents forward of the doors. The two-seater's front clip was almost identical to the 1954 production Corvette front clip. *General Motors*

Chevrolet Nomad
General Motors' first station-wagon-bodied Dream Car was built on a stretched Corvette chassis and powered by the 150-horsepower Blue Flame Six. In 1955, the big brother of this prototype was offered to buyers in a production-version Bel Air Nomad wagon with optional V-8 power. *General Motors*

Choice of an Enthusiast's Enthusiast

Dave Garroway, popular host of NBC's *Today Show* in the 1950s and a noted auto enthusiast and collector, poses with his choice of a 1954 Buick Roadmaster convertible equipped with accessory Skylark spoked wheels. *General Motors*

ABOVE AND LEFT
Erector Set with a Deadline
About 100 hours from start to finish—that's what it took from layout on the Waldorf ballroom to show time on preview night. This five car "cloverleaf" turntable was a Motorama regular for several years in different decors. *General Motors*

CHAPTER 6

1955: Looking at You

In 1955, following the Waldorf showing in late January, the Motorama repeated with a four-city show tour. Miami in February, Los Angeles in early March, on to Frisco in late March, and wrapping it up for an all time first in Boston the last week in April. And what a first time it was, with attendance reaching 594,745 for an all time Motorama record. Attendance for the five-city tour also set a record, topping two million spectators.

"Looking at You" was the theme of the 1955 stage show, as it proved to be another winner produced and choreographed by Richard and Edith Barstow under the direction of the Kudner Agency, producers of advertising for the GM corporate account.

Staging was more spectacular than ever before and incorporated the first major car animation in a Motorama stage. Featuring a two-tier hanging bandstand suspended over a lily pond, the five production cars representing each of GM's auto divisions were presented one at a time via a swinging arm with a turn table on the end, dubbed the "Flying Saucer." Looking like a giant juke box record changer of that era, the arm and turntable were used to present the production cars one at a time, in spectacular fashion. Each production car was loaded onto the saucer back stage, then mechanically raised and pivoted through a string curtain to burst into view like a flying saucer in landing mode. While a narrator described the features, the car spun slowly before the crowd. Following each showing, the arm was retracted and the next car was loaded while the audience was entertained with skits and dancing.

Flying Saucer
Custom constructed for a five-show circuit, this multi-ton mechanical monster required five trucks to transport. *General Motors*

ABOVE AND BELOW
Show Magic
A typical before and after Motorama scene: Boston's Commonwealth Armory on inspection day, and the same building two weeks later. All show materials were flameproofed to meet the Boston Fire Department's requirements. *General Motors*

Seven new experimental cars and a specially designed Dream Truck were the 1955 offerings of Harley Earl and staff. Harlow Curtice explained, "We have given our styling people free rein in developing the new Dream Cars, and the results have been exciting."

The 1955 Dream Cars included the Chevrolet Biscayne, the Pontiac Strato-Star, the Buick Wildcat III, the Oldsmobile 88 Delta, the Cadillac Eldorado Brougham, and two cars developed by GM styling and engineering, the LaSalle II sports coupe and the LaSalle II sedan.

Forget Anything?

When you have hundreds of men working to an unforgiving deadline, you can't afford a holdup because you forgot or can't find a particular bolt. To overcome this problem on the Motorama tour, someone came up with the idea of a "shop truck." Originally not much more than a rolling hardware store, the concept grew to include assorted lumber, steel, plastics, and eventually a miniature machine shop and portable tool room.

Stocking the shop truck became a specialty of its own. Usually the man who would ultimately become its proprietor at the various show sites, was responsible for organizing the hundreds of drawers and cubby holes that lined the forty-foot trailer. Special overhead and under-floor bins and racks stored bulk materials that might be needed. As supplies were used, they had to be replaced as soon as possible to make ready for the next emergency.

GMC L'Universelle
One of the most amazing of the 1955 special vehicles was the GMC L'Universelle, a radio-equipped package-delivery job styled along passenger lines. Nearly a foot lower than conventional panel trucks, the L'Universelle had fully as much load capacity as larger trucks and was designed so as to be adaptable for many uses. Sleek and powerful with front wheel drive, it had a Panoramic windshield and numerous other passenger-car features. *General Motors*

Because of the electric welder and many stationary machines on board, the trailer had to be located where it could be connected to 220-volt shore power. Not a problem in Miami or Los Angeles, but did you ever try to get 220-volt single-phase power on the 49th Street sidewalk behind the Waldorf?

I don't know the cost in dollars to equip and stock the shop truck, but I'm sure it was fully repaid plus dividends after it came to the rescue of some of those after-midnight installation panics.

Anyone Seen Willy?

The only convenient source for laborers and show carpenters in the quantities the Motorama shows required was the New York District Building Trades Council. If you wanted to deal with the union, you met with Willy G. who listened to your needs, and sometimes responded with an occasional nod. I never saw Willy G. travel alone, and when he met to discuss our labor requirements prior to the show, he was usually accompanied by Jimmy V. and several other assistants who weren't introduced.

Jimmy would outline how and where hiring would be done, and Willy would nod when necessary. Jimmy would specify the ladies' room on the second balcony of the Waldorf ballroom as the hiring hall, and then requested its continued availability for use as the union steward's office throughout the installation and dismantling phases of the show.

NEXT PAGES
Pontiac Strato-Star
The Pontiac Strato-Star, a six-passenger two-door hardtop, featured a Panoramic quarter glass on each side in the rear, giving all passengers practically unobstructed vision in all directions. Two narrow cantilever struts in the rear and the front corner posts supported the roof. The low, sleek Strato-Star also featured automatic access panels. As the doors were opened, a paneled portion just over each door automatically raised to allow ample room for entrance to or exit from the car. As the doors closed, the panels automatically slipped tightly into place again. *General Motors*

EXIT

THE DREAM CAR CULT
Memoirs of a Budding Enthusiast—
Bruce Berghoff, Arcadia, Michigan

A chance opportunity to earn some extra college money put me on the shop floor of the George P. Johnson Company in Detroit in the summer of 1951. While I had no prior experience building parade floats, I soon became a foreman directing several other summer employees for the company that designed and produced all of Chrysler's and American Motors' auto shows. The process of being involved from concept to the finished construction of formed-metal structures and finely sculptured wooden forms fascinated me, and the challenge of meeting unforgiving deadlines heightened the thrill.

Following a short military hitch and more auto-show production experience, I learned another local company was producing a series of single-brand multi-million dollar auto extravaganzas, and I wanted to be part of the action . . . and action there was! Cap Stubbs, owner of the H. B. Stubbs Company hired me at first interview and pushed me into the production flurry of the 1955 GM Powerama followed up shortly by the 1956 Motorama.

Materials, money, and excitement flowed in such amazing quantities that rubbing elbows with Dream Cars was almost taken for granted. The high point of sweating around-the-clock production schedules was seeing the black tie, V.I.P. audience queue up outside the Waldorf Grand Ballroom on preview night . . . then share the thrill of their surging through the doors to witness a mixture of forms, materials, lights, and sounds never seen or heard before. This

was show business . . . this was Motorama! After several years of end-to-end shows, one city's streets almost blended into another, but the unique thrill of opening night was always there and the excitement of the show went on.

It wasn't until 1958 that I became aware that something was missing. The show magic seemed incomplete. Some of the luster had disappeared. The Dream Cars were gone! Granted the Firebird III had lots of fins, but not enough pizzazz to make up for the absence of a half dozen one-offs. It finally dawned on me, in spite of all of the fabulous trappings . . . the cars were the real stars, and the prototypes were gone.

This was the turning point that switched me onto cars, very special cars. I refocused my interests into collecting and restoring automotive treasures, which continues to this day.

While most of my retired neighbors spend their days lingering over the local coffee table discussing what the rest of the world is doing, I can't find enough hours to build and provide obsolete parts to an ever-growing international band of antique Cadillac owners.

The cars are still the stars . . . but their owners form a galaxy of friendship that's hard to beat.

I hope some of my enthusiasm in writing these stories will inspire some of you readers to join the legions of The Dream Car Cult!

Bruce Berghoff
M. Reed

On hiring day, laborers were directed to the first balcony where their union badges were checked to see that they were current on dues, and their names were on "the list," whatever that meant. If they passed those tests, they were sent upstairs one at a time to the ladies' room, where Jimmy and an assistant or two presided. I was never told what went on in there, but occasionally saw candidates putting their wallets away as they exited the interview room.

From the beginning of show installation through the packing of the last truck, we never saw Willy G. and rarely saw Jimmy. If a jurisdictional dispute arose on the floor, where frequently five or more different unions were represented, Jimmy would emerge briefly to pass judgment. Otherwise, he remained cloistered in the ladies' room twenty-four hours a day, and on the overtime payroll twenty-four hours a day! After all, what's too high a price tag for the guarantee of no

significant work stoppages on a critically deadlined show program?

Jimmy told me that the fruits of hard work like this had blessed him with a handsome home, a boat at the yacht club, and several nice cars. Maybe sleeping in the ladies' room wasn't so bad after all, but when did he find time to enjoy those perks?

Like Moving an Army

Show props and show cars were moved from city to city on 125 specially equipped and identified semi-trailers. Because of their size and number, it would have been poor public relations on GM's part to have them run in convoy, impeding other traffic, so they traveled in small groups, but were easily recognized by their bold red, white, and blue graphics. Because the show had to be assembled in a particular sequence, somewhat like an erector set or a massive puzzle, accurate truck loading,

Biscayne
Among the design innovations featured on the 1955 Dream Cars was the sculptured styling of the Chevrolet Biscayne. The Biscayne also featured a three-way Panoramic windshield to give the driver greater visibility by extending the windshield above the normal line of vision. The upper third of the Astra-Dome windshield was tinted to prevent sun glare from hindering the driver and passengers. The Biscayne was a four-passenger sedan. *General Motors*

packing, routing, and scheduling was critical. To aid in tracking all of these vehicles, GM used an elaborate radio-telephone network.

Nowhere was the success of this system more important than in New York. Because of freight-elevator limitations at the Waldorf, show materials and cars had to wait their turn between hotel provisions coming in and garbage going out. In a special agreement worked out between the New York police commission and GM, one semi-trailer could be at the freight dock and only one second truck and trailer could be standing-by on a side street. The other 123 trailers were to either be parked in a special parking area in Linden, New Jersey, or they would be in transit between Manhattan and Linden. This was great in theory, but even with the state-of-the-art radio communications, impossible to execute. The added impositions of huge fluctuations in New York traffic, unpredictable winter weather, and the fact that we had only about 100 hours to unload and assemble the Waldorf show, and less time to dismantle and reload the 125 trailers, required some stretching of the rules. Most of the stretching occurred at night when it wasn't unusual to find Motorama vans standing by on every side street within a mile of the Waldorf. Police on the night shift were aware of this practice, and rumor had it that if they visited the show office to discuss the problem they would obtain "satisfaction."

This apparently worked for all parties concerned for a while, but then the word spread to officers on other shifts, and finally to officers from other precincts. It got so bad that we would see uniformed officers arrive at the 49th Street entrance of the Waldorf by taxi, they would complain about alleged truck infractions and ask about receiving "satisfaction" from GM. The next year we were told by GM show execs that there would no longer be an unloading hassle from New York's finest. Seems they had another meeting with the precinct commanders and worked out another agreement, allegedly something providing "satisfaction" for all concerned parties. We were instructed to direct any complaining officers to the GM show office where they would have an appropriate discussion with show officials. Word of this revolution spread quickly among the Manhattan "Blues," but possibly not quickly enough to prevent a few officers from remote precincts to still get burned.

Buick Wildcat III

The only convertible in the Dream Car group was Buick's Wildcat III, a four-passenger job that featured a compound-curved Panoramic windshield designed to lessen the wind problems for passengers riding with the top down. The compound curvature of the windshield greatly decreased the wind problem and added to the new, sporty look of the car.

A novel and efficient air-intake system also was featured on the Wildcat III. The air-intake portals reach the entire width of the car just in front of the windshield and the hood plateau lines extended toward the front of the car from either side of the air vents were parallel, giving a significant appearance of breadth to the front of the car.

RIGHT

88 Delta

On the 88 Delta, a four-passenger two-door hardtop by Oldsmobile, a special treatment of the instrument panel was one of the most intriguing features. A detached horizontal strut extending from side to side just below the steering wheel carried all the instrumentation. Between the strut and the front interior paneling of the car was a four-inch space, which lent a feeling of roominess to the car. The airfoil-type strut also housed a serving tray that could be pulled out from the bottom at the right side. The entire treatment added neatness to the front interior of the car. All wiring was covered along the steering column, a further emphasis on neatness. Another feature of the 88 Delta was the dropping of the beltline from the windshield clear back to the rear window. This added to the low appearance of the car and provided front-seat atmosphere for back-seat passengers. Wrap-around tail lights represented another new feature of the 88 Delta.
General Motors

Cadillac Eldorado Brougham

One of the 1955 Dream Cars was of steel construction: the Cadillac Eldorado Brougham, a sleek four-passenger, four-door sedan. Slightly over 4.5 feet high (54.4 inches), the Cadillac show car represented a significant step forward in GM stylists' endless search for ways to reduce outside dimensions without sacrificing passenger comfort. All seats in the car were individually tailored for maximum comfort, and the two front seats pivoted outward to allow passengers the easiest possible entrance to the car. There was no side pillar to hinder entrance to the rear seats. The Eldorado Brougham had fresh-air intakes on top of the front fenders and outlets in the rear doors. Flush with the body panel, the outlets bore a resemblance to the traditional Cadillac vertical slash. The Eldorado tail fins were among several features that positively identified the car as a Cadillac. Efficient utilization of interior space was one of the most interesting features of the car. All of the Dream Cars except the Eldorado were of reinforced-fiberglass construction. *General Motors*

LaSalle II

Replacing the gas turbine Firebird (star of the '54 Motorama) as the GM entry in the '55 Motorama show-car fleet were two cars, one a two-passenger sports coupe and the other a six-passenger sedan. These twin Dream Cars represent a Harley Earl one-two punch in the styling field. Both bearing the name of LaSalle II, after the original 1927 car Earl designed for Cadillac to start on his way to styling fame, the two cars represent new concepts in auto design. The LaSalle Sedan is an outstanding example of the extent to which GM stylists have been able to combine minimum exterior dimensions with maximum interior spaciousness. While providing all the basic space requirements with respect to passenger comfort, seating, luggage, and mechanical components, the sedan was a small car of 108-inch wheelbase, 52-inch tread, 49.8-inch overall height, 69.5-inch overall width, and 5-inch body-to-ground clearance. The floor, body sills, engine supports, and body shell of the LaSalle II sedan were fused into one integral structure. The body sill housed the exhaust pipe and muffler. It was powered by an overhead cam V-type six-cylinder engine, and had external-type brakes, which featured fine radial blades to help dissipate heat generated by the wheels. The LaSalle II sedan also had an Astra-Dome windshield, similar to that of the Chevrolet Biscayne. *General Motors*

LaSalle II Sports Coupe

The LaSalle II Sports Coupe, the only two-passenger car among the Dream Cars, was also lightweight and minimal sized. The cockpit was well back on the chassis, which had a 99.9-inch wheelbase. Tread was 52 inches front and 50 inches rear, and the height at the top of the windshield was only 42.8 inches. Ground clearance was 5.1 inches. Chassis suspension was independent front and rear, with coil springs at each wheel. It also was powered by a V-6 engine. Styling wise, both of the LaSalle twins carried modernized design features resembling those which made their namesake a hit. Tastefully arranged chrome trim and strategic use of sculptured styling gave the cars the exciting look and graceful lines typical of all the 1955 Dream Cars. *General Motors*

Personalities . . . No Strangers to GM's Motorama
The late Dinah Shore, a frequent spokesperson for Chevrolet Division in the 1950s, did indeed "See the U.S.A. in her Chevrolet" when she attended the 1955 Motorama preview and was warmly greeted by GM's president, Harlow Curtice. *General Motors*

Keep Those Tractors Rolling . . .
Basic to meeting the stringent show installation and dismantling schedules was getting materials delivered on time and
in the right order. A radio-telephone system allowed show
coordinators to keep in touch with drivers on a moment's
notice. *General Motors*

CHAPTER 7

1955: Powerama

Following shortly on the heels of the Boston Motorama, which concluded the tour in May, GM announced its first Powerama, scheduled to open August 31 and run through September 25, 1955. Promoted as the "World's Fair of Power," Powerama was a public show staged in Soldier Field parking lot on the near south side of Chicago. It featured the products and services of GM's non-automotive divisions and showcased diesel power in its many commercial, agricultural, industrial, and transportation applications.

Sharing space on the twenty-three–acre temporarily converted parking lot were:

• The main theme center and display building—Exhibiting diesel research and diesel component equipment plus a Buick jet engine.

• Allison area—Showing various military products in which Allison Division provided engines, transmissions, or servo-drive systems. Included was a VTO (vertical take off) plane, an F-89 jet plane, a guided missile, an atomic gun carriage, and a demonstration of U.S. Army tanks.

• GMC Truck and Coach area—Where the L'Universelle Motorama Dream Truck was featured surrounded by a Scenic Cruiser and Turbo Cruiser bus, plus a variety of on-road trucks.

• Electro-motive area—Where GM's train building division offered a drive-it-yourself engine demonstration as well as other locomotives, mobile power plants, and a Frigifrater refrigerated freight rail car. Popular among the younger set were

For the Benefit of Pilots
Located only 300 yards from Meigs Field airport on Chicago's lakefront, the Powerama theme center building became a temporary landmark. *General Motors*

scale-model locomotives. An additional full-scale model was GM's lightweight streamliner train.

• Euclid area—Products from GM's off-road-equipment division included a fifty-ton mining truck, giant diesel earth loaders, earth-moving equipment, and crawler tractors.

• Fabricast area—GM's precision casting division doing demonstrations of investment casting. This division was initially created to satisfy Buick's need for millions of precision stainless steel vanes, used in the construction of its variable-pitch dyna-flow transmissions.

• Frigidaire—To cater to the ladies, GM reassembled its "Kitchen of Tomorrow" and displayed it with a kitchen of today.

• Detroit Diesel—Probably the division best recognized by a broad segment of the audience and certainly the star of the show, Detroit Diesel power was everywhere. Starting with a demonstration of diesels on the farm, a two-acre field was constantly being worked by Oliver farm tractors. Adjacent to the field was a semi-enclosed functional cotton gin powered by Detroit Diesel. Down the road was a full-blown saw mill, and next to it was a diesel-powered road-building demonstration. But that wasn't all that was powered by Detroit Diesel.

On the Lake Michigan side of Lake Shore Drive was another fifteen-acre show ground. Here, spectators could observe a diesel-powered oil rig, complete with a hundred-foot tower, plus a display of the U.S. Navy submarine *Tautog*, a shrimp boat, a tugboat, and several pleasure boats anchored at dockside—and all powered by Detroit Diesel.

Probably the most popular Powerama spectacle was the huge outdoor stage backing up to a sensational diesel-powered fountain in Lake Michigan. In a crowd-pleasing show produced and directed by Richard and Edith Barstow, GM showed off the precision maneuvering capabilities of it's off-road and on-road equipment. The Barstows were able to combine their Barnum & Bailey Circus background with Motorama stage experience to produce a show that was hailed as "The World's First Technological Circus."

After the crowd was seated in massive bleachers, the circus-clad master of ceremonies cruised onto stage in Harley Earl's favorite machine, the LeSabre.

During rehearsals, I first saw the LeSabre in action and remember thinking it was jet powered. The huge center mounted rear pod was internally illuminated in flashing red lights to resemble a jet exhaust. Not highly noticeable during daytime shows, it was wild at night. I think they broadcast simulated jet sounds during the LeSabre's arrival to enhance the illusion.

Embarking from the Dream Car, the master of ceremonies blew his whistle to summon a mixed fleet of farm and construction vehicles, and gave them their marching orders. One of the machinery acts involved eight Oliver tractors and sixteen western-clad square dancers all performing in the farm-tractor hoe-down.

Symbolic Power
Jeanine Paradine strikes a pose matching the famous Powerama poster. *General Motors*

Continuing, the program included mechanical mastodons, a salute to America's railroads, a ten-girl rough riding troop, the truck fashion parade, and an awe-inspiring aerial act rigged between the extended booms of two diesel crawler hoists. There was more fun with the crawler tractor Mambo, Diesel Dopey the clown, and an outstanding elephant act. Choreographed to the music of *I Can Do Anything Better Than You*, a troop of five elephants were pitted against two Euclid dozers in a series of challenging acts designed to show the mechanical superiority of GM products. Unfortunately, most of the audience was plugging for the elephants, and when the diesels won the crowd moaned.

The grand finale included a musical display of dancing fountains, behind which the program concluded with a giant fireworks spectacular. Sound like a real extravaganza? It truly was, and the only reference to automotive products was the presentation of six of the 1955 Dream Cars plus the Firebird I, originally introduced at the 1954 Motorama.

While the Powerama drew an audience numbering in the millions, it was never again repeated in Chicago or anywhere else.

Don't Break the Windows!

The 300-foot-diameter GM theme center building was the largest of two dozen or so temporary buildings we built in Detroit, knocked down, loaded on trucks and flat bed rail cars, shipped to Chicago, and re-erected on Soldier Field parking lot. While the roof and supporting structure was constructed almost like a panelized modular home, the walls were steel framed industrial sash units consisting of literally thousands of small panes of glass. As a result of rail-car transit and handling in the erection process, several hundred individual panes were broken, but no big deal considering the scale of this operation. A local Chicago glazing contractor was called in about a week before show opening to quote replacing the broken glass. It was no big deal for him either until he notified the local union of his intent.

The Glazier's Union business agent arrived ready for the kill. After all, this was the world's largest auto manufacturer operating against a show opening deadline in a strange town. The business agent wanted to test (and taste) just how deep GM's pockets were.

After reviewing the damage, discovering that the windows came into Chicago pre-glazed by out-of-state labor and that show opening was now only three days away, the business agent made his ruling. "Before the broken glass can be replaced, all of the unbroken panes will have to be removed from the sash frames, reinstalled and cleaned of excess putty." Wow—at his best estimate we would have to put over a hundred skilled union glaziers on the job in order to make opening date, and Chicago didn't have a spare hundred.

I don't know who performed the miracle, but the next day about five men arrived and installed replacements for only the broken panes . . . and the show went on.

Who Was That Masked Man?

The daily arrival of the black on black Cadillac Fleetwood seventy-five sedan with its prominent chrome bumper "bombs" didn't go unnoticed at the job site. The job site after all was the Soldier Field parking lot in the spring of 1955. Winter hadn't been kind to Chicago that year, and the late thaws and abundant spring rains combined with major underground excavations to make a muddy mess. While the Cadillac, actually an eight-passenger limo, didn't look new . . . it didn't look old either; it just looked out of place in the middle of our construction turmoil. Its deep tinted windows obscured the nondescript driver; however, just about every worker on GM's eighteen-acre site looked forward to its visits.

After parking right in front of the stairs leading up to our temporary construction headquarters trailer, a short, overweight, balding man wearing a long black overcoat would exit the spacious rear seat and enter the trailer. Invariably both rear windows would then be lowered in the limo, revealing two of the most voluptuous young ladies that ever hit the streets of the Park District—a redhead and a blonde as I recall. It didn't take many visits for all of us to look forward to the frequent arrivals of Ben Stein and company.

60

Light Up the Night
That was what Powerama did for twenty-six consecutive nights when it hosted millions of spectators. *General Motors*

Stein always started conversations with, "D'ya, d'ya, d'ya need any help taday?" It seemed Ben not only knew his way around the back seat of the limo, he appeared to know everyone and everything going on in Chicago, especially when it came to labor. If we required a special material or skill, Stein knew the source and gladly divulged it. His knowledge was appreciated, and as show opening came closer we grew to depend more and more on Stein's assistance. When asked how we could repay Stein, he would reply, "Oh, oh, I'll tink of somethen" . . . and he did.

When the time came for us to get concerned with hiring grounds porters and toilet-room attendants, Stein was prepared. He could not only take care of the labor, but was prepared to furnish all necessary cleaning supplies, toilet paper, and sanitary napkins . . . you name it, Stein had it covered.

There's More Where That Came From

As prime show contractors to GM, the H. B. Stubbs employees were traditionally provided with a fleet of new, or almost new, courtesy cars in every Motorama town. As an assistant supervisor at my first big GM show, I somehow rated a beautiful red and cream 1955 Bel Air convertible, which really drew attention on the south side of Chicago. I liked that car so much, Cap could have forgotten about the salary, and just given me the use of the car.

After several weeks of Powerama show installation, I had to return to our plant in Michigan for a week, and rather than just lock-up the Bel Air, I thought one of our carpenter foremen might like to use it, and use it he did!

I had heard about the "Official Stubbs South Chicago Headquarters," but hadn't been there yet. This was a bar that opened its doors to Stubbs' fifteen or so visiting foremen with gusto. Even had a sign on the sidewalk welcoming the "Stubbs Crew" and a specially designated parking area in the alley out back, and that was the place my loaner Bel Air was last seen intact.

Seems the boys had such a good party going one night, they walked their ladies to a local motel and left the Bel Air in the security of the alley. Someone in need borrowed the four wheels and tires, as well as the radio and anything else readily removable. The morning rainstorm failed to rouse my entrusted friends to put the top up on the convertible, so the rear well became a rolling fish tank (or would have if there had been any wheels to roll on).

When I returned to Chicago to reclaim my prize I was told of the untimely demise of the Bel-Air and, after accepting the loss, began to wonder about my longevity after GM heard about the tragedy.

Well, my job continued, and I was told GM knew where there were more Bel Air converts.

A Once in a Lifetime Opportunity

At every Motorama, time was the enemy. Unbelievable deadlines had to be met, and someone had to watch the progress and watch the clock to see that the show came together as scheduled. Cap Stubbs was that someone. Cap led his men into battle and they never failed to deliver the goods.

Their performance was the result of loyalty and loyalty was the result of Cap taking care of his men. Regardless of what kind of trouble you got into, Cap came through in a pinch.

Chuck, one of Cap's paint crew, had very little road-show experience prior to the Powerama. Because of the many outdoor structures getting scuffed up in transit and during the erection process, Chuck was sent to Chicago for several weeks to assist in supervising the last-minute painting.

While the hours were long, Chuck still found time to hunt out the south-side action spots and bend an elbow or two. At one such spot he was befriended by a stranger, who after hearing about Chuck coming on a mission from Detroit, asked Chuck's assistance to solve a problem.

We had no qualms about Stein's proficiency on the supply end of things, but judging from his rear-seat companions, we all wondered what his ladies toilet attendants would look like. "Na, na problem, we scr . . . screen 'em," said Stein. And scr . . . screen 'em he did. No one could have provided a more thorough service than Ben.

Several years after the close of Powerama, I met an advertising representative from Leo Burnett's Chicago office who had just taken over GM's Saginaw Steering account. While visiting at lunch, he produced a photocopied booklet that had circulated Burnett's offices supposedly listing the "Who's Who" of Chicago's underworld. Remembering only a handful of characters whom I had met and worked with at the Powerama, I casually studied the booklet until I saw the name Ben Stein, convicted the previous year of labor racketeering and then currently serving hard time.

Euclid Takes a Dive

The immense size of this fifty-ton off-road mining truck built by the Euclid Division was highlighted by converting it into a swimming pool. Frequent diving demonstrations per-formed by lovely young ladies plus clown diving acts kept audiences pressed against the ramp handrails for hours. *General Motors Sales*

Seems the stranger had "found" a large amount of money, but suspected the bills were "marked" and represented a probable threat to anyone circulating them in the Chicago area. Chuck on the other hand did most of his spending over 200 miles away. "How about a two for one deal?" It sounded pretty good to Chuck but he really didn't have much capital to invest.

Returning home one weekend, Chuck disclosed the opportunity to his neighbor, who agreed to invest a significant portion of his savings. After all, you don't get a two-for-one opportunity every day!

Chuck went back to Chicago carrying his neighbor's money, plus whatever he had in his own cookie jar. He found the stranger and an exchange was arranged. Chuck would drive to a well-known downtown location and park, keeping the money in a shoe box. Armed with a description and license number of Chuck's car, the stranger's accomplice would deliver the two-for-one loot in a similar shoe box, and Chuck was to depart post-haste.

All went as planned, and the exchange went smoothly. Chuck even peeked into the box before he raced off, and saw the stacks of currency. Several miles from the exchange site Chuck couldn't hold off any longer. He stopped and fanned the bills. He just about flipped when the stack turned out to be cut from pages of the Chicago telephone book.

Panic set in and Chuck's first move was to call his "investing" neighbor with news of this turn of events. Recovering from the shock, the neighbor advised Chuck to go to the Park Police and report the swindle. The neighbor then phoned the Chicago Police from Detroit and reported that Chuck had swindled him out of his money, without acknowledging the existence of a third party.

The Park Police had lodging awaiting Chuck when he arrived, and Chuck now found himself alone in a squeeze play he hadn't considered. Not knowing a lawyer, and in spite of the middle of the night hour, Chuck immediately called Cap Stubbs. After all, isn't that what a boss is for? Cap listened to the story and assured Chuck he would get some action in the morning.

We don't know how Cap did it, we only know that several days later Chuck returned to work with a very sheepish look.

AUGUST 16 1955

Drilling for Oil
With only two weeks before show opening, the oil-rig crew works overtime. *General Motors*

BELOW
Temporary Rigging
Powerama aerialists put their faith in diesel-powered boom trucks. *General Motors*

CHAPTER 8

1956: Key to the Future

The 1956 version of GM's Motorama became another five-city show. Following the January New York opening, the tour followed the same path as the 1955 shows: Miami in early February, Los Angeles in early March, Frisco in late March, and concluding in Boston in late April.

Another all-time attendance record was set, this time in Los Angeles with a single-day crowd numbering 100,553. While overall attendance for the entire tour went up marginally to 2,348,241, the cost of this production escalated to almost $10 million, and in those days that was a lot of money. In just the New York show the cost per spectator had gone from $3.10 in 1950 to $10.48 in 1956. In today's economy, that would roughly translate to $55.12 per person. How many free auto shows did you attend in the last year that cost the producers that kind of money? A second interesting thought is . . . if GM had given you the $10.48 in 1956, and you put it in your local bank savings account, how much would it be worth today? Providing your bank was still in business, roughly $80.32. This exercise might be a clue as to one of the reasons for the demise of the Motorama after 1961. But on with the show!

"Key To The Future" was the theme of an all-new stage concept choreographed by one of Broadway's greatest, Michael Kidd. Gil Stevens wrote the original music, which introduced the fabulous Firebird II. For the first time on a Motorama stage, GM combined audio-visual effects with live action to totally enthrall its audiences.

The show began with the audience focused on a huge projection screen covering the entire stage set. The panoramic film started by introducing you to the all-

CONTINUED ON PAGE 73

Club de Mer
The Club de Mer by Pontiac the only open-topped Dream Car for '56, this slippery-skinned finned missile stood only three feet high and was only fifteen feet long. Fabricated in aluminum and powered by a 300-horsepower dual-quad V-8, this beauty featured a rear-mounted transmission and De Dion rear suspension. Finished in light metallic blue, the interior was upholstered in crushed-grain Vermilion leather. The Club de Mer remains one of Pontiac's most memorable show cars almost forty years after its introduction. *General Motors*

COLOR GALLERY

1938 Y-Job
Harley Earl's 1938 Buick Y-Job is heralded as the concept vehicle that started the Dream Car era. *Courtesy Buick*

1953 Miami Motorama
Miami was the second stop of a seven-city tour that became the longest in the history of General Motors Motoramas. *Courtesy General Motors*

1953 "Motorythms and Fashion Firsts"
High fashion in evening gowns as well as motor vehicles dominated the 1953 Motorama stage. The $5 million cost to GM confirmed its intent to impress the audience. *Courtesy General Motors*

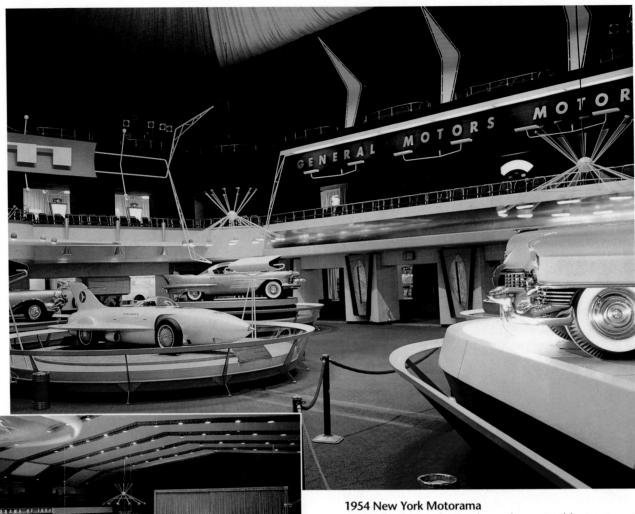

1954 New York Motorama
The Firebird I was featured on a low turntable, to present this Dream Car at an advantageous elevation. *Courtesy General Motors*

1954 Chicago Motorama
The five car "cloverleaf" turntable became the theme center for this first and only Motorama to visit Chicago. *Courtesy General Motors*

1954 Los Angeles Motorama
This heroic billboard over the entrance of the Pan-Pacific Auditorium welcomed thousands of spectators in 1954. *Courtesy General Motors*

1954 Chicago Motorama
Because of its late introduction in 1953, the Corvette was still hot news on the 1954 Motorama tour. *Courtesy General Motors*

1954 Corvair Dream Car
Although this fastback never reached production as a Corvette, the rear clip design might have inspired some later Mustang stylists. *Courtesy General Motors*

1954 Corvette Production and Dream Cars.
The 1954 production Corvette convertible leads a prototype '54 with bolt-on hardtop, the sleek Corvair coupe Dream Car, and the original Nomad Dream Car. *Courtesy General Motors*

1955 Boston Motorama
Staged in the Commonwealth Armory, this old building was literally transformed by General Motors into a showcase of automotive jewels. *Courtesy General Motors*

1954 Nomad Dream Wagon
Another design that never reached production as a Corvette. It took only a year, however, to surface as the 1955 Bel Air Nomad wagon. *Courtesy General Motors*

RIGHT
1956 Pontiac Club De Mer Interior
The most outstanding feature of the twin-cockpit interior was the use of self-leveling seats. In order to give some degree of function to the unusually low windscreens, seats were mounted on rubber diaphragms that compressed under the load of occupants. *Courtesy Sky Van Duyne*

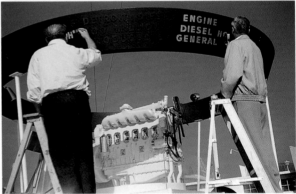

Painters Finish Powerama Theme Center
An army of more than 300 painters was summoned to touch-up exhibit buildings before the public could come in. *Author*

A Beacon Over Key Biscayne
Workers set one of two 150 foot pylons marking the entrance to the 1956 Miami Motorama. *Author*

1956 Miami Motorama
The delicate Aerotent aluminum framework looks like the skeletal structure of a beached whale. *Author*

Workers Enjoy Rehearsal
If the boss is going to watch, there's no sense in the rest of crew working. *Author*

1959 Buick Mirror Display
The multifaceted, mirrored back wall of this exhibit fascinated audiences while enabling them to see the Buick's interior at the same time they viewed its exterior. *Author*

1959 New York Motorama Firebird III Introduction
Continuing the series, Firebird III was touted as refining the outstanding features of Firebird I and II while introducing startling innovations of its own. *Courtesy General Motors*

BELOW
1961 Oldsmobile Display.
Oldsmobile's New York Waldorf display room took on immense proportions through the use of mirrored walls designed by GM Stylists. *Courtesy General Motors*

1961 New York Motorama.
The jewels of the show, top of the line models from each division, grace the "Grasshopper Stage" at the Waldorf show. *Courtesy General Motors*

LEFT
Firebird Hydraulics Repair
The Firebird IIIs multitude of hydraulic servo-systems required regular show maintenance in order to insure flawless demonstrations every hour. *Author*

LEFT
1961 Pontiac Display.
The Tempest Liftbody demonstration (at left) was the featured act in Pontiac's New York Waldorf display room. *Courtesy General Motors*

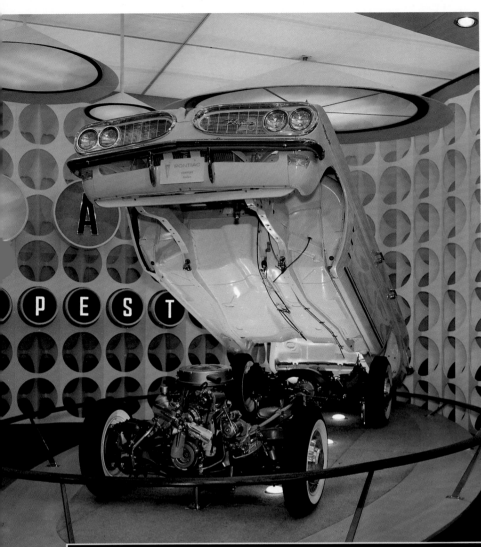

LEFT
1961 Pontiac Tempest Liftbody
To demonstrate the Tempest's unusual suspension design and flexible driveshaft connecting the engine with the rear transaxle, Pontiac's engineers conceived this liftbody display. *Courtesy General Motors*

BELOW
Hail to the King
When his court paid homage to the king in GM's 1961 Motorama stage show, the king presented the cars as the stars. *Author*

Reach for the Stars
Motorama performers go through their steps during a pre-show rehearsal at the Waldorf. This custom stage was designed to enhance the show theme, "Key to the Future."
General Motors

CONTINUED FROM PAGE 64

American family of the future going on a trip: Mom and Dad in front, and their early teenage son and daughter in the rear. Dad, behind the "unicontrol" joy stick begins with a pre-flight check of vehicle control systems, monitored on the instrument panel. When all systems are go, Dad starts the almost silent regenerative gas turbine engine, and the Firebird II is under way.

Headed for a long desert trip, Dad uses the exit from the city to demonstrate the function of the unicontrol. "Press the stick forward to accelerate, left for a left turn, right for a right turn, and pull to the rear for a smooth stop." Having made the family somewhat comfortable with the idea of no steering wheel, Dad now does a run through of this amazing vehicle's other features.

The "Delco-matic" air/oil suspension system used an oil-driven piston to level the vehicle and a trapped air reservoir to eliminate bumps. The central hydraulic system employed a compact, high-pressure hydraulic power supply, which made possible extensive use of hydraulically-powered accessories from a central source. Four-wheel disk brakes came from GM's Moraine Division. A high-output electrical system from Delco-Remy included a transistorized regulator. Reviewing these features on film not only gave Dad an opportunity to promote several of GM's accessory divisions, but it gave the GM Sales Section the ability to spread the cost of developing the Firebird and the Motorama motion picture over several participants.

After plugging the contributors, it was time for Dad to relax a bit. Engaging the autopilot steering and drive system, Dad rotated his swivel captain's chair, invited Mom to do the same and it was time for all the family to play on-board Monopoly as the Firebird II cruised the desert (and hopefully deserted) highway.

Although a lot of this segment was film-maker's magic, I did observe the autopilot system in actual test at the GM Technical Center. With a five-inch-wide metal strip taped down to one of the Tech Center service drives, a modified production Chevrolet was inching its way down the road and very gingerly negotiated a right hand turn before coming to a stop. I heard later that this vehicle, or one similarly equipped, didn't make the turn and

The Titanium Star of the Show
Streaking down the stage highway and screaming to a stop, the self-guided, driverless Firebird II enthralled audiences of all ages. Note the left and right front tracking sensors that homed on the metallic highway strip to guide the automatic steering control. *General Motors*

74

ABOVE AND BELOW
Firebird Mania
In addition to its numerous exterior features, no small attention was given to Firebird II's exotic gas-turbine power plant, its air/oil suspension, its central hydraulic system, and its prototype transistorized electrical system. *General Motors*

dove into the Tech Center reflecting pond. While huge in area, fortunately the pond is only a few feet deep.

Well, back to the film . . . Dad's geographic locator system tells him they are approaching their destination, so it's time to pack up Monopoly and swivel around for a landing. As Dad takes back the controls, the mammoth motion picture screen swings upwards to reveal the actual Firebird II descending a highway curve and coming to a stop almost into the audience. A doorman greets the family, loads their baggage onto a roller conveyor and guides the visitors to a cylindrical glass elevator that whisks them to the second level of GM's fantasy motel of the future. The dancers follow the Firebird down the highway of life in the future and break into song, "Tomorrow, tomorrow all dreams will come true."

As the stage show ends, the narrator introduces the other Dream Cars exhibited in pairs on individual turntables set forward of the main stage.

Who Was That Lady?

Having several years and numerous shows' seniority on me, my show supervisor partner Gerry Russello had his choice of night or day shifts during show set-ups, with me getting the shifts he declined. The New York show had to be installed in about 125 hours, and these ran around the clock because of the high Waldorf building rental costs. The labor crews would work twelve hours on, and then twelve hours off, with a replacement shift coming in every twelve hours, so the work went on uninterrupted. So that we could keep each other informed of problems and progress, Russello and I worked the twelve hours on plus an overlap hour making for five contiguous thirteen hour days (or nights) as the case might be.

While I originally thought getting the night shift was a raw deal, I soon discovered I couldn't tell night from day anyhow, as there were no outside windows in the ballroom or the other show rooms. The only way we distinguished night shift from day shift was that there were fewer GM corporate "sidewalk" superintendents around changing their minds on the night shift.

One evening, as I hailed the Waldorf elevator to begin the midnight shift, I was joined by three GM styling-staff executives and their ladies. I hadn't met their wives before, but proceeded to introduce myself to the ladies, calling them by what I presumed to be their last names . . . while the execs all looked a little sheepish.

I was later prompted to forget that evening, attributing the "illusion" to having worked so many consecutive thirteen-hour shifts.

What's the Hold-Up?

"Pre-installation," that period when the erection of general show-place ceilings, wall drapes, projection booths, and outdoor plantings and signage took place, was a fairly leisurely operation. All hell broke loose starting about a week or ten days before show time. That's when trucks start rolling in by the dozens daily, and labor crews can't be standing around waiting for materials to be unpacked. Loading-dock space is at a premium, and the army of fork lifts must be orchestrated in concert with the master unloading

Two by Two
Dream Cars filled the Waldorf ballroom, but production cars were relegated to the back rooms. *General Motors*

76

Cadillac Eldorado Brougham Town Car
Featuring a padded rear roof upholstered in polished black leather and an open top over the front seat, this four-door Dream Car revived the town-car styling reminiscent of some limited-edition Cadillacs of the 1930s. Built on a 129.5-inch wheel base, this show car stood only 55.5 inches high. *General Motors*

Buick Centurion
Powered by a 325-horsepower version of Buick's production V-8 engine, the Buick Centurion featured a closed-circuit TV in place of a conventional rear-view mirror. To free up driver's-side leg room the steering column was located on the centerline of the dash and incorporated a cantilever-suspended steering wheel inspired by aircraft design. For the convenience of front- and rear-seat passengers, the front seat automatically moved forward to allow rear-seat entry and backward to facilitate front-seat entry. *General Motors*

list. As trucks are called, they are instantly emptied and moved out . . . or should be. It's not much different from keeping an auto assembly line going. A stoppage can cost big bucks.

Well, one afternoon at Dinner Key Auditorium in Miami someone asked me what the hold-up at the loading dock was all about. Charging down there I saw the back end of a closed car transporter and lots of GM brass holding a meeting. Investigation disclosed the Club de Mer Dream Car had arrived from New York with a sheared axle. Some GM engineers had the car jacked up within the trailer, and didn't want to move it or the trailer until a new axle shaft could be flown in from Detroit. I could see myself explaining a ten- to twelve-hour hold-up at the loading dock to Cap . . . No way!

Without investigating any further I ran to the front of the auditorium, where I had a crew welding an entrance sign together. I quickly explained the problem to "Brownie" and he took off with the arc welder in the back of his old truck headed for the loading dock.

Oldsmobile Golden Rocket
Like the Centurion, The Golden Rocket offered mechanical assistance to ease entry and exit. When either door was opened, a roof panel retracted, and the seat raised and rotated toward the driver or passenger. Tilt steering was introduced to further assist driver entry. With its sleek metallic-gold-finished flowing skin, the golden rocket utilized a 275-horsepower Olds Rocket V-8 engine. *General Motors*

When I sent Brownie over to look at the axle, I didn't give much thought to the rumors that hung a quarter million price tag on each dream car. Brownie didn't look, dress, or act like a musician, but he was a real maestro when it came to striking the torch. I sometimes worried about the smell of booze that always seemed to accompany him, but he had after all, hung the steel in the ceiling of Dinner Key Auditorium without mishap.

Pretty soon, Brownie returned to finish the sign frame without comment. When I asked his opinion about the axle he just said, "It's taken care of." I didn't ask any more about it and he didn't tell me . . . but the car came off, and the truck moved away from the dock.

Several months later I encountered one of the GM engineers who had been involved in the axle incident. He asked me how we happened to have a welder on the job in Miami, knowledgeable and equipped to weld titanium. "Who . . . Brownie?"

I guess the old adage might be right, "What you don't know won't hurt you," but I sometimes wonder how many heads would have rolled if Brownie had torched the Club de Mer and its trailer into extinction, in front of all those engineers.

He Went That Way

Selling glamour . . . with glamour was not a new concept to the auto industry, but Buick took it to new highs at its 1956 Motorama exhibit.

They featured a one-off Roadmaster convert with pearlescent peach upper and cream lower paint finish, and custom matching leather interior set off with peach dyed mouton carpeting. The real grabber was two evening gowned plaster mannequins flanking the raised and tilted car.

The model on the left wore a necklace identified as . . . "Brazilian-Portugese emerald-cut diamond—Value $125,000; Emerald-cut ring—Value $225,000." The model on the right wore jewelry identified as "The Hope Diamond—Value $1,000,000; Marquise-cut diamond ring—Value $75,000." Although the signs credited

Harry Winston Jewelers with the loan of the stones, I was never certain if these were "gennies" or fakes. But to add to the illusion, two uniformed and armed guards were posted discreetly, but partially visible behind the "eyebrow" of the display.

One rainy night at the Boston Motorama the building lights suddenly went out. Fortunately there had been power outages before, and the Armory had been equipped with battery powered emergency lights, but not many of them. Our first concern was getting the crowd out of the building safely. Not long after this was accomplished, power was restored, and the overhead lights came back on.

While it hadn't dawned on us, several of GM's exhibit crew were certain this outage was a plot to steal the Buick diamond display, and we instantly descended into Buick's exhibit to check it out.

The diamonds were fine . . . but there was no sign of the guards!

Flying With the Greatest of Ease

Bob Eaton, my industrial design instructor at Wayne University, left academia in 1954 and joined H. B. Stubbs Company as chief designer. Bob created the concepts for most of the non-Motorama clients for whom we built trade show exhibits between Motorama assignments, and because these fill-in jobs were vital to maintaining the core work crews between the big shows, Eaton was rarely invited to join us out on the tours. He was essential doing what he was doing.

As a reward for his steadfast efforts, Cap Stubbs asked if Eaton would care to leave Detroit at the height of winter and assist us in Miami for two weeks. Anticipating his answer, Cap had already purchased the airline ticket and made motel arrangements. Eaton would fly out of Willow Run Airport Saturday morning, arrive Miami early afternoon, enjoy the weekend at poolside, and be ready for work Monday morning.

Eaton beamed his approval and accepted the airline ticket and travel advance. When he broke the news to his young family, he couldn't resist inviting his wife Becky and their three children to join him. After all, the almost new Henry J could still gallop, and this opportunity for togetherness would make up for some of the late hours Eaton had spent working. Gas money wouldn't be a problem; he could cash in the airline ticket, and with his expense money they could even eat.

The plan was to pack the kids in the back seat Friday after school and head south immediately. There were no interstates in the 1950s, but Eaton had it figured that with an all-night Friday head start he would only have to cover about 500 miles on Saturday and again on Sunday to put him into Miami well before reporting time Monday morning.

He pledged Gerry Russello and me to secrecy, knowing Cap wouldn't want anybody on the job that hadn't slept, or slept much, in three days.

Well, Monday arrived, but as far as we knew Eaton didn't. We called the motel, and Eaton hadn't

Picture Me Behind the Wheel
This youngster fantasizes himself cruising in this GM styling scale model of a possible design for the future. *General Motors*

checked in. Cap came around about 10:00 A.M. and we knew there would be questions, so Russello and I took off in different directions. By 11:00 A.M., still no Eaton, but Cap nailed us with the inevitable. Our answer, "He's around here somewhere," didn't hold Cap off for long.

We stalled through the lunch hour, and when Cap returned at 1:00 P.M. and still no Eaton, we knew the jig was up. "So what's the story boys?" asked Cap. Russello said he thought he had heard Eaton say something about driving down so he would have a car here. I agreed, and nothing was said about Eaton's family coming. After a few choice comments, Cap left us alone the rest of the day, and we continued to worry about Eaton and his family.

Tuesday morning, Eaton showed up looking like he hadn't slept in a week. With his sly grin he told of driving the Henry J where no car had traveled before. It seems that some time after midnight on Friday, somewhere in Ohio, Eaton didn't see the Detour sign. He wasn't sure if he had dozed off, but he came wide awake after crashing the barriers and flying the car over the end of the pavement. With his headlights buried into a dirt bank, it took a while to figure out just what happened, where they were, and if everyone was all right. It took longer to find help.

Saturday morning, after the Henry J had been lifted back onto the roadway and towed to the local

NEXT PAGES
What Happened?
But what about today's cars? Well, if you stretched your neck to the rear of the room you might find some. Actually, this was the first and only Motorama that didn't feature consumer available passenger cars on stage. It might just be coincidence, but GM's domestic and world-wide vehicle sales dropped over 20 percent between 1955 and 1956. Sales continued to drop for the next two years, which might have inspired GM's sales gurus to put production cars back on stage in 1959. *General Motors*

I Can Get It for You Wholesale
One of the features that prompted me to buy this '56 Bel Air
show car. *General Motors*

gas station, it was determined the car needed some
suspension parts. Eaton's story about probably losing his job, plus three crying kids prompted some
action, and the J was back on the road by Saturday

After seeing Eaton's haggard looks, Cap didn't even bother getting an explanation; he already knew Eaton's creativity extended far beyond the design studio.

(Eaton and I were to team up under the name Design Origins, Incorporated six years later to form our own exhibit design, construction, and service company. He retired to Florida in 1982 where he rejoined H. B. Stubbs as a contract field supervisor on GM's Epcot program. Eaton died suddenly in 1984, shortly after the public had recognized GM's Epcot exhibit as a winner.)

New Kid on the Block

While on my first solo assignment in Miami shortly after joining H. B. Stubbs Company, I became annoyed at the lack of gusto shown by some of my southern labor crews and reported my frustration to the boss, Cap Stubbs. Cap listened politely and then imparted one of his famous jewels of wisdom by telling me, "You have to learn to laugh in this business . . . or you'll never make it through the first show." What I didn't know at the time was that Cap had these crews on a time and materials contract with GM, and the slower the crews, the greater the profit for H. B. Stubbs. Cap might have been laughing all the way to the bank.

Several weeks later a jurisdictional dispute arose between two unions working on my job. Not having prior experience negotiating with unions, I invited the respective business agents to a meeting, provided them with doughnuts and coffee, and promptly left the meeting with a parting statement that they could call me when they resolved the problem . . . in that I wouldn't have a vote anyhow. Well, it didn't take them long to come up with the answer. All we had to do was use the same number of men from both unions. They expected I would hire extra men to balance the crews; instead, I fired some to create the balance. Not exactly what they had in mind!

Shortly after this unscheduled layoff, I noticed a man hanging around our show site talking with other men on the work crews. He appeared for two or three days before I asked him his business. He responded that he felt the panels we were hanging in the ceiling of the Dinner Key Auditorium were unsafe and posed a serious threat to the public. When I discovered he had been one of the men recently laid off, I asked him if he would feel differently if he were back on the payroll. Without hesitation he assured me the ceiling would be much safer, and I politely invited him to leave the building.

The next day, he reappeared with a reporter from the *Miami Herald* in tow, and loudly recited his accusations. I consulted the city safety inspector and at his suggestion retained a private engineering consultant to perform tests on the building structure and render an opinion on our work. We passed with flying colors, but not before the newspaper came out with their story headlined "Disgruntled Laborer Stops Show Work."

The next day, Cap called and went ballistic in reprimanding me for threatening the future of the whole show. I should have stopped with my explanation of how I got the crews back to work, but no, I had to

night. This time, Becky laid down the law, and there wouldn't be anymore after-dark driving. Following this plan put them in Miami about 7:00 A.M. Tuesday.

Worth a Million or More
Buick added several million dollars to the value of their Roadmaster convertible with the addition of some choice gems. *General Motors*

remind him of his recent bit of wisdom: "You have to learn to laugh." Luckily, I survived the explosion that followed and learned my second bit of show biz wisdom in the process: Never repeat Cap's jewels back to Cap!

Princess Who?

The yacht that tied up sometime overnight at the Dinner Key Marina Dock had to be over a hundred feet long. We couldn't help but notice it when we arrived one morning to continue taking out the Motorama show. I had to get the crews started just then, but there would be time at noon to look her over.

About mid-morning the word started circulating among the men that the Prince of Monaco captained the vessel, and Princess Grace was on board. I wasn't totally surprised because I had heard stories about Motorama attracting all sorts of celebrities. If presidents were Dream Car buffs—why not princes and princesses?

Shortly before noon someone reported that a statuesque blonde was sighted on the top deck in a scanty

swim suit. That was all it took for several of us to hustle over to dockside to get a closer look.

We didn't spot the Princess, but did have a chance to marvel at her beautiful craft. She was at least a hundred feet long, with lots of glass and polished chrome. Topping the second deck was a wide teak rail and a line of probably a dozen outboard motors perfectly lined up in order ranging from very small to super large. There were only two life boats up there, so we decided the extra outboards were just backups in case of an emergency. If you were Prince Rainier wouldn't you be prepared?

We kept our eyes on the yacht for several days but only spotted the blonde again at a distance. One way or another we were going to see Princess Grace before we left town.

In scanning the *Miami Herald* the next day, I spotted a photo of the Prince's yacht, but the caption said it belonged to Ralph Evinrude, the Milwaukee manufacturer of Johnson and Evinrude outboard engines. That explained the line-up of outboards clamped to the second deck rail, but what was he doing with Princess

Making a Splash in Miami
The huge water-filled fifty-ton off-road mining truck by the Euclid Division proved to be such a hit at the recently concluded Powerama show that it was brought to Miami, complete with bathing beauties and their supporting clown act. *General Motors*

Grace on board? Well the story went on to tell about Evinrude and his wife, Frances Langford Evinrude, having arrived to attend the Miami Boat Show.

That good-looking blonde was none other than the famous Frances Langford, big band singer of the 1930s and Bob Hope's lead songstress during numerous World War II U.S.O. tours. Who needs Princess Grace with Frances Langford around?

Just Plain Lucky

Following some of the tour shows, GM would make slightly used show cars available for purchase to the show staff and crew. It was not unusual for our carpenter foremen, rich with tour-acquired overtime pay, to pick up a fully loaded Buick or Olds with surplus cash and drive it back home to Detroit to surprise "Momma."

Not blessed with a union mandated time-and-a-half and double-time compensation plan, my supervising partner, Gerry Russello, and I had wallets that dictated more pedestrian tastes. That gray and white Chevy Bel Air hardtop caught my eye, and Russello preferred the same model in turquoise and white, so at the end of the Boston show we struck a deal.

A slight problem . . . we were told we couldn't have the cars until Saturday afternoon, and Cap was expecting us back in Detroit on the job Monday morning— and what Cap expected, Cap got!

The plan was to get loans and temporary insurance riders from Detroit, plates from Boston, and pick up the cars Saturday noon at the delivering Chevy dealer in Cambridge, leaving us a day and a half to make it back to Detroit. (This was 1956 with one-and-a-half lane mountain roads and no freeways.)

What really happened was . . . the motor vehicle bureau in Boston wouldn't honor our Michigan insurance rider and wanted us to purchase a full-year policy issued in Massachusetts. Not to be stopped, we hot-footed it up to Rhode Island where insurance wasn't required. Using the same fictitious address in Providence, we purchased consecutively numbered plates, returned to Cambridge to pick up our new twin cars, and begin the marathon drive back to Detroit.

ABOVE AND RIGHT
Quick-Change Kitchen
Contrast the photo of Frigidaire's 1949 Motorama "Kitchen of Today" with the 1956 Motorama "Kitchen of Tomorrow." In Frigidaire's "Kitchen of Tomorrow" the miracles never ceased. In a film produced to promote the '56 Motorama, GM showed a typical housewife loading that domed oven with ingredients for a cake, slipping into a tennis outfit, then a golf dress, and finally a swim suit and returning to find the cake done, complete with frosting and candles lit. Come-on GM . . . do you think they believed that stuff? *General Motors*

Having lost about four hours in pursuit of plates, we had some time to make up. Two hours on the winding mountain roads running about seventy miles per hour when we could, found us only 100 miles into our trip. It also found us in the hands of a western Massachusetts version of "Sheriff Buford." He was cruising the mountains in an unmarked dirty black 1940 Chevy coupe when he spotted the twin show cars up front, and he knew he had struck gold. I was the lead car when I spotted the coupe (coming up fast) in my mirror. The plain-Jane vintage Chevy fooled me until he pulled into oncoming traffic, got broadside of my left window and motioned me over with the largest black pistol I had ever seen. When I stopped, he lined Russello up behind me and the questions started.

"Lemme see . . . you got driver's licenses issued in Michigan, car purchase receipts from Cambridge but your plates show a home address in Providence, and you both live at the very same address. You guys sure get around . . . around seventy-five through a thirty-five-mile-per-hour-posted small town."

After scanning our papers, and listening to our story about possibly losing our jobs unless we returned to Detroit by Monday morning, Sheriff Buford just scowled at us. He finally broke the silence with, "Either you two are the unluckiest jerks or the two dumbest crooks I've ever met . . . I shoulda locked you up but I'm lettin' ya go so Michigan can have ya."

Things went well after that until we arrived at Canadian customs inspection, crossing into Canada at Niagara Falls. We told them we hadn't purchased anything, but when they found two boxes of liquor in our cars we had to explain. It seems some of our Boston contractors had a departure party for Russello and me, and presented us with a number of fifths. I explained that neither of us drank much, and assured them that all the bottles would remain sealed as we cruised Highway 401 to Detroit. The two customs officials were unconvinced, and insisted on confiscating the booty. I could almost see them drooling over this prize. I didn't want to corrupt (or further corrupt) government officials, and remembering a distant relative who lived nearby in North Tonawanda, I made a phone call. I could see the officials faces drop as I recited a detailed inventory. Aunt Helen and Uncle Morris enjoyed my phone call for many months, and toasted Russello and me often . . . and we made it to Detroit and kept our jobs.

CHAPTER 9

1959: Imagination in Motion

Between the close of the 1956 Motorama five-city show tour and the opening of the 1959 Motorama, GM's domestic auto sales shrank almost 20 percent. Buick's sales nose-dived to its lowest full-production-year level since 1939, and the only car division to show an improvement since the last Motorama was Pontiac, spurred by the arrival of Semon "Bunkie" Knudsen as general manager, Pete Estes as chief engineer, and John Z. DeLorean as the new director of advanced engineering.

The overall dismal performance of the other car divisions probably impacted the corporation's decision to limit the 1959 Motorama to showings in New York and Boston. Even with this reduced schedule, attendance at both cities dropped almost 20 percent, while cost per show attendee shot up to an average of $7.63 per head, probably raising thoughts of a limited show future amongst corporate bean counters.

After the catastrophic sales fall-off of 1956, followed by dismal sales results in 1957 and 1958, five slick production cars, one from each of the car divisions, were back on stage in the 1959 Motorama. Featured in a thirty-five–minute stage show titled, "Imagination in Motion" was a cast of 100 performers including the June Taylor Dancers, made famous on the early Ed Sullivan television shows.

The center of activity was the ninety-five–ton "grasshopper" animated stage mechanism. Following a short fantasy film depicting "Imagination in Vehicles," the June Taylor Dancers introduced each car line in song and dance. With each introduction, the huge grasshopper arms delivered one production car up and over the audience for a brief spin, and then retracted behind a barrier to await the finale. The stage

More Than a Dream Car
The Firebird III was touted as a racing laboratory of future GM vehicle advancements. *General Motors*

Crowd-Pleasing Entertainment
Opening with a fantasy-trip color motion picture, the thirty-foot by sixty-foot projection screen magically tilted upward to reveal a second level orchestra, under which each of the five car divisions' products were unveiled with the assistance of a full-blown dancing troupe. *General Motors*

show ended with five cars spinning. With three cars high, two low, the orchestra blaring, and the dancers kicking, the audiences roared with approval . . . but would the cars sell? Well, buyers started spending and GM showed a 30 percent domestic sales improvement over the next three years.

Firebird III

"Imagination in Motion," the show's theme, also carried over to the introduction of the Firebird III, touted as refining the outstanding features of both the Firebird I and II while adding startling innovations all its own in the field of human engineering. Conceived as a joint effort by GM's research labs and the styling staff, with cooperation of the engineering staff and many participating GM divisions, the corporation was careful to point out that Firebird III was not a Dream Car, but it was a practical workshop for testing advancements that could well improve your GM car for the next few years.

Let's see how accurate its forecast was:
• The ultrasonic key—just aim it at the door and the door sweeps open . . . not bad for starters.
• Formed plastic interior—color is not merely a surface coating but is integrated uniformly throughout the material . . . score two for the home team.
• Unicontrol steering, shifting, accelerating, and braking—a complete absence of steering wheel, shift lever, brake pedal, and throttle . . . whoops, they didn't score too well on that.
• Simplified instrument readings—including tell-tale warning lights . . . they sure came through with that one.
• Autoguide—An electronic guidance system that automatically steers the car . . . some of today's cellular phone users think they have this feature.
• Cruise control—automatically holds the Firebird at a pre-selected speed . . . this feature was already available on production Cadillacs.
• Automatic headlight switching—a light sensitive panel that switched on low-beam and high-beam units

with diminishing daylight . . . this was an upgrade of GM Guide Lamp Division's Autronic Eye, which had been available as a production option for almost ten years.

• Advanced temperature control—allowing pre-set warming or cooling of the cockpit *before* the car is occupied . . . probably killed by the threat of unattended in-car fires.

All in all GM didn't fare too well on its forecast of features to become available in the next few years. Even so, thirty-five years later we're still waiting for some of the Firebird III's more spectacular advancements.

Perhaps a clue to the reason for this delay can be found in the power story of the Firebird III. GM called it, "A unique dual-power system complementing the gas turbine engine with an important non automotive concept—the accessory engine." That's right, the Firebird carried a completely separate two-cylinder, ten-horse-power gasoline engine to power the electrical and hydraulic accessory and control requirements of the many on-board systems, whether cruising or parked with the main engine turned off. In addition to the combined weight of this servo engine, hydraulic pump and

generator plant, was the bulk. Completely filling the front engine compartment, it forced the primary turbine engine into the rear, effectively eliminating any trunk or storage area. Even the spare wheel was eliminated, but GM said from the beginning that this was a test car with no pretense of being a family sedan. So much for the impractical, let's look at the real powerplant.

The Whirlfire GT-305 rear engine was a 225-horse-power regenerative gas turbine with no other demands than to propel this laboratory on wheels. Coupled to a Hydra-Matic–type transmission mounted directly to the differential case this De Dion trans-axle arrangement drove two short driveshafts with universal joints. With a curb weight of 5,275 pounds, no performance figures were published or even discussed outside of GM's research and engineering labs.

Brakes were of major interest to inquiring enthusiasts after they heard the weight statistics, and brakes were something that GM's engineers also didn't neglect. Called the Turbo-Al (Turbine-Aluminum) system, it featured a primary braking unit in which the wheel and

The Flying Five
Crowds were amazed as the all pearlescent white production cars were hurled from outer space almost into the audience.
General Motors

Glamour Abounds
The cast of 100 June Taylor Dancers dazzled GM's guests hourly. *General Motors*

drum were combined in a single aluminum casting with thirty-six cooling air passages. Sprayed-metal rubbing surfaces on the drums and sintered metal linings provided wear resistance and positive action, even when wet.

Additional braking was provided by a grade retarder mounted on the rear of the differential. Through a series of friction discs, the retarder provided braking torque on the rear wheel drive-shafts.

A third braking feature was the introduction of the 1959 version of antilock brakes. GM called the wheel speed sensor device "a magic box" that automatically evaluated premature wheel slowdown and maintained proper line pressure to prevent brake lockup.

Supplementing these devices were three air-brake flaps at the rear of the car. They opened automatically in conjunction with the grade retarder on downhill runs to direct air through the Firebird's oil coolers. While it's questionable that the Firebird III ever attained very impressive speeds, we are certain it came to a sudden stop.

Other Motorama Cars

Divisional Motorama vehicles for 1959 included primarily production cars touting new and wonderful

engineering and styling features. Pontiac introduced "wide-track" chassis design with a tipped-over Pontiac display showing normally hidden chassis and drivetrain innovations. Buick and Olds capitalized on their all-new body lines. Chevrolet put its emphasis on a slick new passenger-style pickup named the El Camino, a vehicle obviously inspired by Ford's Ranchero, which had been introduced two years earlier.

XP-74 Cyclone

A Dream Car mystery that remains to this day is the XP-74 Cyclone. Built in 1958 by GM's styling staff, apparently in plenty of time for introduction at the 1959 Motoramas, it didn't appear publicly until late February 1959 and then under the name Cadillac at the Daytona, Florida, "Speedweek." Because the Cyclone's body lines resembled those of a diluted Firebird, the Cyclone's designers were said to be suffering from "fin fever." Huge, shark-like fins protruded upwards from the rear fenders, offset by more subtly finned skeg moldings on the lower body. The Cyclone was powered by a rear-mounted production 325-horsepower V-8 engine coupled to a three-speed transmission, and the

Loaded with Innovation
The multi-purpose "unicontrol" includes single-hand steering, shifting, accelerating, and braking. *General Motors*

Cyclone's exhaust was funneled through two massive, trailing jet tubes. Bearing rear fin logos identical to those appearing on the Firebird I of 1954 Motorama fame, it is possible that XP-74 might have been intended as a continuation of the Firebird line, but discarded and re-identified as a Cadillac when corporate brass decided it didn't incorporate enough engineering innovations to be the standard bearer of its '59 Motorama theme "Imagination in Motion."

A second Cadillac mystery model in 1958 was a series of five slightly modified production Eldorado Biarritz convertibles. They all featured a custom fabric top that raised automatically when rain or humidity triggered a sensor. When in the down position, the top was completely concealed by a flush-fitting metal deck. These models were specially prepared for the major auto show circuit, but no record was found indicating their presence at the 1959 Motoramas.

Cars by the Damsels of Design

Prompted by a sales staff that started to recognize the significant influence that women exerted in the selection of the American family car, Harley Earl began to seek women designers to add to his styling staffs. Traditionally, Earl had several females in the Frigidaire product studio to consult on the design of appliances, but this was a new ball game. Not many women had been welcomed at Art Center, California's Mecca for young car designers in the 1950s. Nor were there many focusing on automotive design at Detroit's Society for Arts and Crafts, which didn't get serious about automotive design until the 1960s when it was renamed Center for Creative Studies. Undaunted, Earl went to Brooklyn's Pratt Institute, long recognized in the field of fashion design. Here, he could have the pick of the crop and offer them pioneering opportunities in his almost all-male design studios.

Offer he did, and the women were eager to follow him back to Detroit. Much to the chagrin of the good ol' boys (who for the most part weren't very old), he not only offered the women prime space, but he encouraged them to create a fashion show of feminized cars. Referring to the ladies as his "Damsels of Design," Mr. Earl stated, "They have won their spurs with this 1959

Mighty Midget
Though relatively small, the Firebird III's accessory-drive
engine effectively eliminated any on-board luggage
space. *General Motors*

Any Room for Passengers?
About two-thirds mechanism and one-third cockpit (by volume) or nine-tenths mechanism and one-tenth people (by weight) effectively describes the Firebird III. *General Motors*

collection," and that collection became the feature for the 1959 Motorama.

The Fancy Free Corvette by designer Ruth Glennie not only featured a metallic silver, olive, and white leather interior, but also included four sets of slip covers geared to change with each season.

Jeanette Linder created the Chevrolet Impala Martinique. Perhaps inspired by African costume designs, she incorporated a pastel striped interior with matching fabric-clad fiberglass luggage.

Peggy Sauer accented her Oldsmobile's metallic rose exterior with a red and black leather interior. Possibly to emphasize the Olds' affordability, she added tasteful plaid wool inserts to the leather.

Two Buicks were created by Marjorie Ford. First was the Shalimar. Styled for the career woman of the 1960s, it included a swing-out dictating machine in the glove box and a removable cosmetic case in one arm rest. Her choice of exterior paint was royal purple.

The second Buick by Ms. Ford featured a flaming orange exterior with concealed interior compartments for a removable radio, binoculars, and a camera.

Sue Vanderbilt completed the group of Damsels of Design. Her entry was the Cadillac Eldorado Seville Baroness. Complementing the black ivory exterior was a black mouton fur carpet and sealskin-clad pillows and lap robe for the comfort of rear-seat passengers. She also had numerous built-ins including a personal phone for the baroness.

The Damsels of Design had made their mark before millions of admirers nationwide, and Mr. Earl had made his point with dozens of disturbed male designers. Shortly before his retirement from GM in 1959, Mr. Earl stated, "I believe the future for qualified women in automotive design is virtually unlimited . . . I think in three or four years women will be designing entire automobiles."

To offset the fact that no traditional divisional Dream Cars had been produced for 1959, GM engaged

THE DREAM CAR CULT
Tracer of Dream Cars—Bill Warner,
Jacksonville, Florida

For a guy who never attended a Motorama, Bill Warner has probably seen more Dream Cars than most of the show attendees.

Warner relates: "I became infatuated with the Motorama cars as a child—I'm fifty-one now—and recall chasing the Maryland Cadillac Le Mans down the streets of D.C. in 1957 and pursuing it until last year when I found its home . . . only to find it was sold two years earlier for a bundle. I have visited the Bortz Collection in Highland Park, Illinois; the Sloan Museum in Flint, the Henry Ford Museum in Dearborn, and the Pebble Beach Concours D' Elegance in order to see these cars in the flesh. I have been pursuing the Oldsmobile F88 III for years in hopes of finding it and adding it to my collection. Although I

never was fortunate enough to attend a Motorama, I have been fortunate enough to see a large number of the cars. I sustain my interest in that I am a basic car loony."

In addition to running a full-time industrial filter business, Warner owns Race/toration, a shop specializing in race-car restoration. As a part-time staff member of *Road & Track* magazine, he has photographed and written about numerous cars worldwide.

Warner's current collection of nine unusual street and track vehicles ranges from a '57 Eldorado Biarritz Convertible to the ex-works Lotus II LeMans #209 driven by Graham Hill and Cliff Allison.

Bill Warner
B. Berghoff

Dream Car in Disguise?
This non-Motorama Dream Car is still being shown at the Cadillac Motor Car Museum in Warren, Michigan. *Cadillac Public Relations*

OPPOSITE
In Case You Don't Believe It
Pontiac hung their Bonneville convertible upside down to display their "wide-track" chassis. *General Motors*

in some fancy double talk. Featured in newspaper ads and posters was the following ad copy:

"Excitement about GM Motorama has been building up for days. You can feel it in the air! Everybody knows that this year the cars, the show, in fact everything is brilliantly different. This year's Motorama is going to top them all. You'll see GM's revolutionary new line of design for '59 as applied to Chevrolet, Pontiac, Oldsmobile, Buick and Cadillac sleek new shapes, stunning new bodies, Vista-Panoramic windshields—all dream cars that you can buy and drive, and all on display together for the first time. You'll see the fabulous Firebird III, the experimental car with a new concept in automotive control systems. You'll enjoy a magnificent stage spectacular produced by Maurice Evans. You'll see many fascinating exhibits presented by GM Divisions, and Research and Engineering. So make plans now to attend."

Now "dream cars" became "cars you could buy and drive" and the Firebird III became an "experimental car."

No One Told Bob

The last day of show set-up was always hectic. When we should have been down to polishing brass

doorknobs, we usually found ourselves knee-deep in electrical problems. Ordinarily we had until early evening to iron things out before the V.I.P.s arrived for the black-tie, champagne, and hors d'ouvres show preview. Chances were that they would spend more time looking at each other than looking at the displays anyhow, so we knew we could fake our way through if necessary.

But 1958 at the Waldorf opening turned out to be different. President Eisenhower had arrived in New York, ticker-tape parade and all. I remember hanging out my hotel window as "Ike's" open-topped Lincoln cruised 49th Street. In spite of the Lincoln, or maybe because of it, GM's brass was able to snag Ike for a special Motorama showing. The Secret Service cased the ballroom, balconies, and arcades in advance. Ike and his entourage were to arrive some time before noon of preview day. The Secret Service gave orders that the entire second floor would be cleared of all personnel starting forty-five minutes before Ike's scheduled appearance. I don't think "Mamie" came along . . . or maybe she just wasn't into glitz; regardless, this was going to be a big event.

Things went according to schedule, or they seemed to, until Ike entered one of the divisional display rooms. Sticking out from under a show vehicle were two big boots, with a body attached. The Secret Service went into action, and soon had extracted the intruder while Ike was hustled off to safety.

Damsel of Design
Peggy Sauer demonstrates her vanity case concept for an
Oldsmobile 98 Holiday. *General Motors*

Big Bob Murray, one of Stubbs' foremen, had never
been manhandled by the government before, probably
hadn't been touched by anyone for a long time at least.
Murray explained he was just going about his job of
installing grease-drip diapers to the show cars to protect
the carpets. He had been under cars all morning and
nobody told him Ike was coming.

When "B" Doesn't Follow "A"

Sometimes the demands of GM's show challenges
forced technological changes in our display building
processes . . . like necessity being the mother of invention.
Such was the case in 1959 when the numerous hydraulic
systems on board the highly sophisticated Firebird III
leaked all over our newly finished turntable platform, and
turned the lacquer painted finishes into shaving cream.
After several weeks of research, we found a then-new finish
called epoxy paint that could be pigmented white, would
bond to wood, and was resistant to leaking hydraulic fluid.
The only drawback was that a "hardener" had to be mixed
with the resin to force it to air dry, and unless sprayed
quickly and the equipment cleaned immediately, it would
totally destroy our spray guns and hoses. As this was all very
experimental, the chemical company supplying the finish
had not yet prepared labels to put on the five gallon drums
they shipped to us . . . they merely stenciled "Part A" on
the resin cans and "Part B" on the hardener.

Not many days after we received delivery of about ten
five-gallon drums of the stuff, but before we had a chance
to use any of it, "Pappy" Blair, Stubbs' long time paint
foreman, reported five gallons of Part A missing. Pappy was
not easily flustered and had a *sly* sense of humor. He suggested we not make a fuss about the loss, even though this
stuff was very expensive. He predicted he would expose
the culprit in short order, and in short order he did!

It wasn't long after summer rolled around that one
of Stubbs' carpenters came to Pappy with a strange
story. Seems as how one of his neighbors had painted
his garage two weeks earlier with some white paint
that wouldn't dry. Supposedly the neighbor had tried
heat lights and hair dryers with no success. Blowing
dust and bugs had begun to accumulate all over the
freshly painted walls and the owner was at his wits
end. Pappy asked about the brand of paint, and when
the carpenter replied that it was only marked "Part A,"
Pappy just smiled . . . a lot!

One Good Turn Deserves Another

Boston's Commonwealth Armory was an interesting place to stage a show. Probably built in the 1910s
or earlier, this nearly 100,000-square-foot relic was
used by the Massachusetts National Guard as a training facility, and from every appearance, National
Guard training was not very popular around Boston in
the 1950s. The building was unimpressive outside and
reeked of motor oil and truck fumes in its dungeon-
like interior. In order to accommodate the massive
lighting and electrical demands of the Motorama,
arrangements were made annually with the local power
company to bring in huge transformers to bolster the
meager resources of the building.

In 1958 GM contracted for a completely new
portable show floor system that consisted of plywood
panels clad with a high-quality gray commercial carpet.
They called the panels "carpet squares," although they
were obviously rectangular and not square. GM's show
office insisted we thoroughly clean the armory floor
before installing the carpet squares. Some serious money
had been spent on the new system, and GM intended to
use these carpet squares for many shows spread over
many years.

The Armory floor was old, partially deteriorated
black-top that harbored years of accumulated dirt,
grease, and chewing gum. After trying industrial vacu-
ums, road sweepers, and a variety of scrubbers to no
avail, we opted to seal the dirt into the black-top rather
than try to remove it.

We located a great liquid sealer, and were advised
to use regular paint rollers on long handles for the
best application. We scheduled floor coating to begin
on a Saturday morning when our ceiling hanging
chores could be temporarily halted. We were ready to
go with our crew when the painters' union business
agent arrived with rule book in hand. He asked us to
read his lips as he read, "No commercial painting can
be done with rollers . . . brushes are mandatory." The
program was delayed for several days while a compromise was struck allowing special dispensation for the
use of squeegees . . . and the beat went on!

The rental agreement between GM and the
Commonwealth of Massachusetts was another interesting bit of government wisdom. I understand GM's
lease only covered the main floor marching area con-

Careful of the Turntable Finish
Your author (bottom center) supervises the positioning of Firebird III on its turntable at the Waldorf. Note the special protective "bras" for each fin. *General Motors*

sisting of about 80,000 square feet, leaving no space for show offices, first aid, contractors' offices, press rooms, and so on. While there were several rooms surrounding the marching area, plus numerous anterooms and dungeons spread around the dark catacombs of the armory, the various National Guard tenants said these rooms belonged to the individual part-time training units and would have to be negotiated separately with each tenant.

Apparently, these individual entrepreneurs teamed up and met the right-minded GM officials, and a deal was struck. I was led to believe the military boys enjoyed their new television set and repaired pool table so much, they couldn't wait for the next Motorama to return.

Stopping to Smell the Roses

Typically, the arrival of a Motorama show in town created bonus business for several dozen contractors and literally thousands of hours of employment for hundreds of skilled, semi-skilled, and service-provider employees.

These shows brought prestigious opportunities, and the money wasn't bad, either.

As the general show contractor, H. B. Stubbs Company was responsible to seek out, or sort out, qualified subcontractors to provide everything from hundreds of tradesmen on a moment's notice to service organizations who could keep toilet paper and paper towels supplied and uniformed attendants in every toilet room. The first time around was naturally a learning process for each subcontractor, but as the show returned in subsequent years, a relationship grew and, I suspect, profits followed. Soon, the word got out, and contractors, as well as some opportunists, got in line to get a part of the action.

When Gerry Russello and I arrived in Boston to begin 1958 pre-show preparations at the old Commonwealth Armory, we found numerous phone messages waiting as we checked in to the Beacon Street Motel. Most of the large-volume contracts had already been let, but we had delayed selecting some of the smaller suppliers, and several of our messages were from eager candidates.

One, we discovered upon returning the call, was from a very demanding individual who would settle for nothing less than being awarded the floral contract for the show.

Cut flowers and potted plants were a big deal at the Motoramas. General Motors' styling staff would pre-specify hundreds of species, colors, and even sizes of foliage to be used on stage and in specially designed and built planter boxes around the vehicles and exhibits. They documented complete specifications on drawings, and we found contractors who could deliver and maintain these plants at each city. Because many tropical plants were called for, costs for these plants ranged from several thousand dollars in Florida, where tropical was the norm, to over $10,000 in the northern shows where tropical plants had to be imported in heated trucks.

We agreed to provide each potential floral contractor with a bid and specification list after they provided credentials about their green houses, and abilities to provide plants in the quantities and time frames we required.

Well, it turned out the "demanding" prospect gave us false credentials on his facilities. He didn't think two kids from that hicktown called Detroit would ever investigate greenhouses in greater Boston. As I recall, this prospective contractor didn't even have an office. Anyhow, we politely thanked him for his interest and told him we couldn't consider him for this year's show . . . but come again sometime.

He responded by telling us he was the brother-in-law of a local Chevrolet dealer who had told him to "go pick up the contract." He also was sure we had accepted a bribe from the winning contractor, and this was going to be reported to GM's president and board of directors immediately.

Our flowers were exceptionally nice in Boston that year, and the president must have enjoyed them enough to overlook the accusations.

CHAPTER 10

1961: The End of an Era

Blocking out major show space at U.S. convention cities had to happen many months in advance of intended use. Undaunted by rather poor attendance and very high per-person costs at the 1959 Motorama, GM made preliminary plans for a five-city tour for the winter of 1960–61. Following another opening in New York would be stops in San Francisco, Los Angeles, Dallas or Houston, and a wrap-up in Miami or Miami Beach.

While the 434,000-unit increase in GM's domestic car sales in 1959 reinforced by an additional increase of 700,000-plus sales in 1960, were not enough to bring U.S. sales back up to the level enjoyed in 1955, 1960 became the second best sales year to date in GM history. Nonetheless, GM's conservative management cut show budgets and two cities leaving a show tour of New York, San Francisco, and Los Angeles

To further conserve on budget, GM reused the grasshopper-arm stage mechanism of 1959 and eliminated the production costs of a feature motion picture. The stage-show cast was cut from more than 100 dancers in 1959 to a modest, but beautifully costumed team of twenty-nine performers. In a highly colorful series of medieval skits written and produced by Gil Stevens and Bob Haymes, the cast sequentially introduced five 1961 production cars to a background of live music and flying sets.

As if to celebrate the demise of the Motorama Dream Car, GM brought the Firebird III back for a last curtain call rather than build something new and spectacular. The focus was on production cars, and GM wouldn't let the audience forget it.

The "consumer available" product theme in cars was furthered in the Frigidaire exhibit. Breaking a long-running "Kitchen of Tomorrow" tradition, GM

It Takes a Lot of People
There were almost as many directors, producers, writers, choreographers, costumers, and musicians behind the scenes as performers on stage.
General Motors

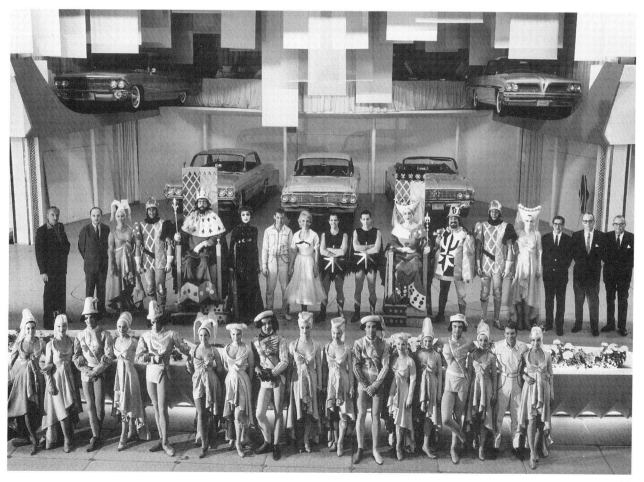

Twirl Those Beauties
Even though the grasshopper stage had been seen before, it continued to enthrall audiences. *General Motors*

chose to show only appliances currently available through any Frigidaire and Delco Conditionaire dealer

General Motors had turned the corner on publicly revealing innovation and the death knell tolled for future Motoramas.

A Weighty Decision

The Motorama stage mechanisms that presented GM's five car lines to an ever expectant consumer audience were masterpieces of engineering. Incorporating a blend of mechanical, hydraulic, and electronic ingenuity, I often thought GM should eliminate the decorative concealments and house the mechanisms in clear plexiglass so the audience could appreciate the works. In retrospect, my critics were right . . . GM was selling automobiles, not stage wizardry!

No staging was more spectacular, however, than that conceived for the 1961 Motorama. On the "grasshopper" stage," five cars were mounted side-by-side on individual turntables. The three center turntables were mounted on four-legged rising grasshopper platforms, while the two flanking turntables were on elevator arms

on rotating columns. Delivery of the cars was choreographed to music and staged to reveal one car, retract it and deliver the second, and so on in sequence until the fifth car was featured. Then all five vehicles sprang forward and twirled, three at stage level and two elevated because of ballroom width limitations.

The geniuses who built, operated, and serviced these huge devices were the Sedor boys . . . Andy and his big brother Bill. Their company was known as Anchor Conveyor, and as the name implies, they weren't only involved in the glamorous pursuits of show business, but when the opportunity knocked, they were ready to work their magic with steel.

The grasshopper stage used plenty of steel, and all of it had to be assembled piece by piece on the second floor of the Waldorf. Rumor had it that this was the biggest and possibly the heaviest mechanism yet to grace the Grand Ballroom.

I didn't give it much thought until one or two nights before show time. Getting on the elevator with me were the Sedor boys. When we arrived at the main floor, I asked them to join me for a drink in the lounge just

Your Chariot Awaits Milady!
Although in a bit of a time warp, the show kept the audiences attention. *General Motors*

across the lobby. They thanked me but said . . . no way were they going to walk through the lobby . . . *no way!* I was puzzled until the next day when I realized the ballroom stage with the heavy grasshopper mechanism was directly above the Waldorf lobby.

What's That Smell?

No one ever said show biz was going to be easy . . . and it rarely was. In order to display a vehicle on the mezzanine of the Waldorf, cars were brought to the second floor (ballroom) level and carefully ramped and winched down two flights of marble stairs. It seems the architects never dreamed the hotel would be used for auto shows, and when they began, GM worked around the physical problems.

This process never improved, and in 1961 while attempting to lower a pre-production Corvair Greenbriar Sportswagon into the Frigidaire "Ideas for Living" contemporary home display on the mezzanine, disaster struck. Having made it halfway down the first flight of stairs, the rigger foreman was informed that work on that project was going to stop for the day, while

other trades continued with their jobs on overtime. The crew proceeded to block and tie off the Corvair for the night.

Much to our surprise (but possibly not everyone's) morning found the nose of the Greenbriar buried into the marble wall, and several bronze handrail stanchions demolished.

It became the corporate decision to continue moving the vehicle down to the mezzanine, while replacement sheet metal was ordered flown in from Detroit. A local GM dealer set up a body shop in the Waldorf and repair and repainting was completed before show time.

General Motors' headline describing the Greenbriar setting read . . . "It's a garage . . . a workshop . . . an outdoor living room" to which someone commented . . . "but smells like a paint shop!"

"Rattlesnake" Strikes It Rich

The arrival of a GM show in town attracted many "official" as well as "unofficial" characters to the showplace. One of the best loved "semi-official" characters on the Motorama circuit was "Rattlesnake Pete" Jack

THE DREAM CAR CULT
Up the River to Motoramaland—
Sky Van Duyne, West Bloomfield, Michigan

Hanging out at the local bump and paint shop on Saturday mornings might be the custom of the hot rod set, but would you expect to find business executives in their early fifties there? That's where I first met Sky Van Duyne in 1984 and discovered that we shared Motorama experiences. Van Duyne recalls:

"My interest in cars and auto shows began in the 1950s when I was in my early teens. Since my family lived near Manhattan, my dad took me to the Motorama one year, and that experience ignited my future enthusiasm for Dream Cars. Dad and I attended Motoramas in New York City for several years, but 1961 was the first time that I hopped aboard the Lackawanna railroad at the Glen Ridge, New Jersey, station, rode to Hoboken, took the old Hudson Tubes under the Hudson River into New York City, and walked uptown to the show

by myself. That was also probably my first trip to New York City without my dad, and I was only fifteen years old."

Van Duyne took his new Bolsey B 22, 35mm Set-O-Matic camera and concentrated on shooting the Dream Cars. While he can't remember how he was able to arrange for the Dream Car doors to be opened, he has interior photos of most of the cars, and still uses the camera more than thirty years later.

Van Duyne's boyhood exposure to the Motorama shows, and particularly the Dream Cars stimulated a love for unusual vehicles that prompted his owning a number of sports cars over the years. While his career is not automotive related, he maintains his car passion through building and collecting car models.

Sky Van Duyne
S. Van Duyne

Balanger, an old time electrician who somehow knew more about the electrical secrets of some old show buildings than anyone else around. Regardless of which contractor was given the Motorama show electrical work, he would be almost helpless without the assistance of Rattlesnake Pete on the payroll . . . so Balanger joined us annually under the auspices of a variety of employers.

Curious about the name, I asked Balanger its origin. It seems electrical work was slow during the depression so he supplemented his income by hunting rattlesnakes in the Florida Everglades, and the state paid him a modest bounty. He apparently did enough better than his competition to pick up the name "Rattlesnake," but I can't recall how Pete got tacked onto the end.

When he ran out of rattlesnakes, Balanger traveled the dog racing circuit. He went from the East Coast to the West Coast following his favorite dogs, which Balanger called "Doaggies." His luck wasn't real good at the tracks in the beginning, so he learned to wire up the mechanical rabbits to finance his habit. He became so good at wiring, tracks started chasing Balanger and for lack of a regular home address just asked for "Rattlesnake Pete" on the dog track circuit. He eventually settled in south Miami not too far from the dog track, and somehow his luck with dogs changed dramatically.

Never having gone to a dog track before, I was thrilled when Rattlesnake invited me to join him on what he described as a rare outing one evening. Explaining that his old legs didn't work well enough to climb the steps down to place a bet, he invited me to do his running. For the first six races I placed two-dollar

bets on the dogs of his choosing, and for the first six races he lost his two dollars. On the seventh race Rattlesnake gave me twenty dollars to bet, and for the first time that evening he sent me back to pick up his winnings, which were substantial as I recall. That was a great evening for me, and it was good enough for Rattlesnake that he asked me to join him again the following week.

Are You Dizzy Yet?
When the grand finale hit, eight, count them, eight production cars whirled to the music. *General Motors*

102

Cadillac Eldorado Biarritz Convertible
As featured in Cadillac's Motorama display, this car was downgraded in 1961 to become almost indistinguishable from the less-expensive Series 62 model. *General Motors*

History repeated itself, and Rattlesnake consistently lost on his two dollar wagers, but struck gold on his single twenty dollar bet.

After the third week, I finally asked him his secret. "Why no secret at all," Rattlesnake replied. "I just go down to the cages before the first race and talk to the Doaggies! They tell me how they're feelin, and I have my answer on how to bet." Rattlesnake must have listened well because he hit on every twenty dollar bet the rest of my winter trips, but apparently his frequent conversations with the "Doaggies" weren't always with the knowledge of his fine wife.

The night I was invited to his home for dinner, his wife said we were celebrating because Rattlesnake had made an infrequent visit to the dog track the night before and brought home fifty dollars. I thought it strange that this should thrill her. After all, he normally hit for between $100 and $200 dollars when we went—but why hadn't he invited me to do his running?

I later discovered Rattlesnake had two or three young friends like me, who each had an assigned night to run his weekly wagers. If the I.R.S. was watching they never saw Balanger at the cashier's counter, and his wife probably thought all that money came from overtime pay . . . after all, "Rattlesnake Pete" didn't spend many evenings enjoying home-cooking.

NEXT PAGES
Buick Flamingo
It was attractively mirrored to reveal modified mouton carpeting, silk paisley upholstery, reversible front seat, and custom pearlescent orange paint. *General Motors*

Are We There Yet?
Buick's modified Electra 225 convertible, featuring a passenger seat that could be faced rearward, made the audience chatter. *General Motors*

Pontiac Bonneville Convertible Coupe
This production convertible became the division's Motorama feature, despite the availability of the high performance one-off Monte Carlo Tempest, which was unveiled at 1961 consumer auto shows. *General Motors*

Chevrolet Impala Convertible
Introduced as "a special car from the world of fashion," this
convertible with a custom interior became Chevy's feature
vehicle. Management apparently voted down showing the
experimental Cerv-I, which made a big splash in earlier auto
shows. *General Motors*

Technical Demonstrations
General Motors' engineering and research displays entertained and informed millions of spectators. *General Motors*

Mechanical Marvel
The show audience missed out on seeing how a stage was
assembled. *General Motors*

CHAPTER 11

Why Did the Motoramas Die?

In the beginning, starting with the prewar Industrialist's Luncheons and expanding into the open-to-the-public Motoramas of the early 1950s, GM was successful in taking its message to selected audiences at a predictable cost.

The audiences were targeted from demographic or geographic information. Demographic in the case of the Industrialist's Luncheons when GM concentrated on important banking and financial people. These were fairly obtainable targets because most of the powers were headquartered on the east coast and a single gathering at New York's Waldorf Astoria Hotel brought them together.

By the late 1940s when the public's war-created auto demand began to be satisfied, GM's concept of creating additional consumer demand in selected geographic areas proved successful. The Motoramas were a perfect marketing vehicle to present a broad array of automotive and household products to a regional market. GM enjoyed a captive audience, and the spectators were treated to an exciting and extremely entertaining experience.

So what went wrong? Costs for one thing! Prices for building shows, trucking, space rentals, installation, and dismantling escalated tremendously in the immediate postwar decade. On the show scene, GM became known as "Generous Motors." Some contractors as well as labor awaited the opportunity to take advantage of deadline threats in order to intimidate extra monies from GM. After all, the show must go on regardless of

Can We Spend Money or What?
Over $8 million were spent on exhibits and displays within their Futurama building. *General Motors*

Care to Wait Awhile?
It took police to keep this army of potential spectators in line as they waited to sweat inside Boston's Commonwealth Armory. *General Motors*

cost. General Motors' sales department tracked these expenses over the years and its data indicated that the show's cost rose from an average of $2.75 per person in 1949, to $7.63 in 1959. That's almost a 300 percent increase in a ten-year period when GM's domestic-car sales volume, as well as share of market, showed only modest increases.

Something else was going wrong: Harley Earl's concept of getting public reaction to advanced vehicle designs at public shows. Not only was the feedback informative to GM researchers . . . but Ford and Chrysler loved the opportunity to get detailed product information as well as the public's reaction to it. The competition's only cost was a couple of airline tickets and a few nights' hotel room and board. No wonder the competition could deliver new designs cheaper than GM.

Changing consumer attitudes were also affecting the future of GM's Motoramas. Some past show attendees were recalling the long lines, crowded halls, and uncomfortably high temperatures and then decided to stay home.

The lush displays, extravagant showplace decorations, and splashy stage shows were having a reverse influence on a segment of those that did attend. They couldn't help but wonder about the costs of these extravaganzas and who was paying the bill . . . perhaps they were?

But the final blow came as the 1961 Motorama was drawing to a close. GM sales executives were offered what appeared to be another golden sales opportunity, the 1964–65 New York World's Fair. But what started out as an opportunity soon became a competitive challenge. Ford announced plans for major participation, and Chrysler was soon to follow. General Motors had enjoyed a relatively captive show audience with its Motoramas, but a World's Fair in the heart of the domestic marketplace on a level playing field was a potential threat to GM, not an opportunity.

GM however, was staffed a step ahead of Ford and Chrysler. They had a battalion of Motorama show planners, designers, architects, and engineers already in place.

THE DREAM CAR CULT
A Glowing Career Kindled by Dream Cars—
John Gunnell, Iola, Wisconsin

"My interest in the GM Motoramas springs from a love of auto design. I studied industrial design at Brooklyn Technical High School in the early 1960s. This was shortly after the last Motorama, but still in the Fisher Body Craftsman Guild era. I also saw the GM Dream Cars at the 1964–65 Worlds Fair in Flushing Meadows, New York. Those were probably the last show cars, until relatively modern times, to really embody the Motorama Mystique.

"I never did enter the design field, but ultimately earned a degree in fine art and went on to become an automotive journalist and historian. The first story that I had published was about a plexiglass-bodied 1940 Pontiac made for the New York World's Fair in those years. Through my collecting and club affiliations, I became involved with writing about vintage Pontiacs and Pontiac Motor Division's many Motorama cars. I have done four Pontiac books titled, *75 Years of Pontiac-Oakland, 1969–1973 Trans Am Photo Facts," Illustrated Firebird Buyer's Guide*, and *Illustrated Pontiac Buyer's Guide.* Currently, I work as the Director of Editorial for the books department of Krause Publications in Iola, Wis. This company produces *Old Cars, Old Cars Price Guide,* and automotive books.

"My friend Al Sico restored the 1953 Pontiac Parisienne Motorama car, which is my personal dream machine. I would love to drive this open-front town car, the first Pontiac town car ever built, to some ritzy hobby event. Another friend, Joe Bortz, now has this car, plus three or four other Pontiac concept vehicles. Like Joe Bortz, I think these cars are very special. They are what the 1950s were all about in terms of vision and perception."

John Gunnell
Old Cars Weekly

To face the challenge, GM would shelve any future Motorama plans and shift its focus to the World's Fair. Its show battalions were increased to army size, and a competitive battle ensued.

General Motors far outclassed its domestic competitors in New York from April 1964 through the fall of 1965 with its highly successful Futurama, which portrayed "Many Minds and Many Hands Serving the Needs of Mankind."

How would they top this success in the domestic marketplace? Would a rekindled Motorama tour make the grade? How could GM get its message to targeted consumers in a timely and cost-effective way?

There were many questions . . . and fortunately, many answers. The world of communication had exploded since the last Motorama.

Regional newspapers and national magazines had created demographic editions. Advertisers could pick their markets and send specific messages directly to those markets at a fraction of the cost necessary for national coverage.

To bolster revenues, theater chains offered motion picture spots to advertisers and another targeted opportunity to a captive audience was created.

But the real biggie was network television. Not only could GM reach a massive audience at the cost of a fraction of a penny per viewer, they could do it with the flair and drama of a trade show and without the inconvenience. Weather would be eliminated as an attendance factor. They didn't have to worry about labor disputes at the showplace or truck breakdowns between show sites.

Life could be beautiful without Motorama . . . and it was! But what happened to the concept of Dream Cars?

Motown's new way of doing things has been getting lots of press recently. And what is that new way? It involves consulting consumer groups as to their likes and dislikes in vehicle design and features. Sometimes, as in the recent Ford Mustang redesign, several different prototype vehicles were built and shown to a core group of historic Mustang club members, a dealer council, and some general consumers. From the feedback, preferences were tallied and final design criteria were established.

Working with an internal product-development team consisting of representatives from engineering, manufacturing, marketing, accounting, design, dealers, suppliers, and workers who built the car,

Building Anticipation
General Motors kept the public informed on its World's Fair
progress through the publication of regular press releases.
General Motors

Ford set records in bringing this consumer driven product to market.

Well, isn't the beginning of that process somewhat similar to what the Motorama Dream Cars were all about? Granted many of the Dream Cars reflected Harley Earl's personal preferences in style and color, but he and his staff listened to the comments and watched the reactions of Motorama audiences very carefully. Concepts like wrap-around windshields, quad headlights, pivoting bucket seats, and numerous styling refinements went right from show floor to production cars as a result of Mr. Earl's Dream Cars.

Did this involvement of consumers in the design process die with demise of the Motoramas? If it didn't, it sure went underground for a long time. Cars of the 1960s and 1970s sprang from the industry's attitude that it knew better than the consumer, what the buying public wanted to drive. Essentially, the marketplace was asked, "Do you have any problems to fit these solutions?" This was somewhat a continuation of Henry Ford's Model T days when he offered his car lines in any color the customer wanted . . . as long as it was *black*.

While today's press touts the customer-driven design process as the "new way of doing business," Harley Earl would probably counter with "What goes around comes around."

CHAPTER 12

Where Are They Now?

As each generation of Dream Cars completed their Motorama tours of duty, some saw action at national and regional public auto shows; others took up brief occupancy in GM building showrooms and divisional lobbies.

When their day in the sun was over, some of the fabulous works of art were relegated to a GM-leased warehouse on Detroit's northeast side. Here, they joined dozens of retired styling "bucks" of prototypes or production designs no longer needed on a day-to-day basis by the corporate styling studios.

At the request of GM's legal staff, individual trim, mechanical, and electrical components were selectively removed from some cars to be used in corporate litigation to prove "prior art." As parts were removed, they were replaced with tags indicating date removed and destination of the missing parts. Unfortunately, many of these parts never returned, and some Dream Cars took on the appearance of porcupines because there were so many tags dangling.

I remember one of the early, functional Dream Cars that was pressed into service by GM styling as a delivery van, carrying mail and drawings to various plants and offices. It was so neglected it didn't even rate a wash job.

The warehoused "porcupines" remained until sometime in the late 1960s, at which time GM discontinued its warehouse lease, and the cars were either destroyed or dispatched back to their respective car divisions or corporate staffs.

The paths these cars took from 1970 to the present are probably interesting and diverse, but mostly unknown to the author. With the assistance of collector/restorer

1951 Buick Le Sabre
Buick's 1951 Le Sabre dream car is now owned and exhibited at the Alfred P. Sloan Museum. *General Motors*

1938 Buick Y-Job *Drawing by Bob Eng*

Bill Warner of Jacksonville, Florida, and writer/historian Don Keefe of Farmington, New York, I have been able to assemble the following schedule of the whereabouts of some Motorama Dream Cars:

• 1938 Buick Y-Job—Still owned by GM and now on long-term loan to the Henry Ford Museum in Dearborn, Michigan.

• 1951 Buick LeSabre—Owned by GM and also on long-term loan to the Henry Ford Museum.

• 1951 Buick XP-300—Owned by and exhibited at the Alfred P. Sloan Museum in Flint, Michigan.

• 1952–53 Corvette—After Motorama it was allegedly used as a factory "beater," then rebodied as a test bed for the 1955 production V-8.

• 1953 Pontiac Parisienne—Found in New Jersey and restored, now in the collection of Joe Bortz, Highland Park, Illinois.

• 1953 Oldsmobile Starfire—Seats owned by Floyd Joliet of GM, vehicle allegedly destroyed by GM.

• 1953 Buick Wildcat I—Allegedly, two cars were originally built. One is now in the Joe Bortz collection, and the fate of the second is unknown.

• 1953 Cadillac LeMans—Possibly four were built originally. One was sold to shoe magnate Harry Karl, customized by George Barris, and subsequently burned in a garage fire. A second was purchased by Floyd Akers, a Washington, D.C., Cadillac dealer and recently sold to a collector in the D.C. area. A third is owned by Jack Goodman of Los Angeles and was restyled in 1959, supposedly by GM for Mr. Goodman's father. A possible fourth LeMans was traced to an owner in Ohio in the early 1980s, but its current whereabouts is unknown.

• 1953 Cadillac Orleans—Unknown.

• 1954 Firebird I—Currently owned by GM and stored at the GM research-staff facility.

• 1954 Corvette Nomad and Corvair Fastback—Both were allegedly scrapped by GM, however it is rumored that the Nomad was stolen

1951 LeSabre

1951 Buick LeSabre *Drawing by Bob Eng*

THE DREAM CAR CULT
Dream Car Writer—
Donald J. Keefe Farmington, New York

Automotive writer and historian Don Keefe became interested in Dream Cars at age four, when his father brought him to the now defunct Hallman Chevrolet in Rochester, New York. It was there that an old experimental Corvette was on display. When no one was looking he snuck under the rope and slid behind the driver's seat. "I remember being scolded by a salesman," Keefe recalls, "but I also remember thinking that it was worth it."

After graduating from St. John Fisher College in 1986 with a Bachelors Degree in Communication/Journalism, Keefe began full-scale research on Motorama and other American nonproduction vehicles from the 1930s to the present. It was at that time that he began communicating with the historical departments of every GM division, as well as those of Ford and Chrysler.

In 1988, he was hired by CSK Publishing as an associate editor for *High Performance Pontiac, High Performance Mopar, Vette, Musclecars, Bracket Racing U.S.A, GM Enthusiast,* and *Muscle Mustangs & Fast Fords* maga-

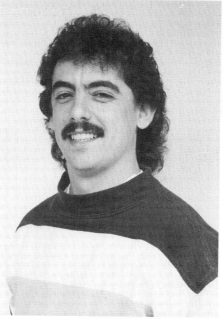

Don Keefe
D. Keefe

zines. He worked his way up to the senior editor position of CSK's *High Performance Pontiac,* where he instituted the popular "Department XI" series. Department XI was devoted to Pontiac's experimental and Dream Cars, giving historical background as well as current information about the surviving cars.

As a result of Department XI, he has written several articles about dream car collector Joe Bortz and the Bortz Classic Dream Car Collection, which he regards as one of the highlights of his career. "Joe and Marc Bortz have done an amazing job of preserving these cars for future generations," said Keefe. "The mere fact that they have amassed such a collection is nothing short of miraculous."

Keefe is currently the executive editor of *Pontiac Enthusiast* magazine and is currently working on a series of articles chronicling Pontiac's Motorama heritage.

---

and is in storage in a California warehouse.

• 1954 Pontiac Strato Streak—Rumored to have been destroyed by GM in the late 1950s or early 1960s after touring the major auto-show circuit.

• 1954 Pontiac Bonneville Special—Two were built, one for the Motorama shows and one for the Pontiac dealer circuit. Both were recently in the Joe Bortz collection.

• 1954 Olds F-88—Possibly as many as three bodies were built. One was partially destroyed by fire, and various rumors persist about others leaving GM as gifts or in pieces. One survivor is known to have been restored in Arizona and sold at auction to the Blackhawk collection in Danville, California.

• 1954 Olds Cutlass—Unknown.

• 1954 Buick Wildcat II—Currently owned by and exhibited at the Sloan Museum.

• 1954 Cadillac Park Avenue—Unknown.

• 1954 Cadillac La Espada and 1954 El Camino—According to GM sources, these cars were destroyed by GM.

• 1955 GMC L'Universelle—Unknown.

• 1955 Chevrolet Biscayne—Recently in the Joe Bortz collection.

• 1955 Pontiac Strato-Star—Unknown.

• 1955 Olds 88 Delta—Unknown.

• 1955 Buick Wildcat III—Scrapped by GM.

• 1955 LaSalle II Roadster and Four Door—Both were rescued from a Michigan salvage yard several years ago by Joe Bortz and the Roadster is being restored.

• 1955 Cadillac Eldorado Brougham—Unknown.

• 1956 Firebird II—Currently owned by GM and stored at the GM research-staff facility.

• 1956 Chevrolet Impala—Unknown.

• 1956 Pontiac Club de Mer—A Pontiac division historian believes it to be in Oklahoma or in the Salt Lake City area in rough shape. Others think it was scrapped.

• 1956 Oldsmobile Golden Rocket—Rumored to be in a New Jersey collection, but not confirmed.

• 1956 Buick Centurion—Alive and well at the Sloan Museum in Flint, Michigan.

• 1956 Cadillac Eldorado Brougham Town Car—Recently in the Joe Bortz collection.

• 1959 Firebird III—Owned by GM, it is on long-term loan to the Henry Ford Museum.

• 1959 Cadillac Cyclone—Owned by GM and now on permanent display at the Cadillac Historical Museum, Warren, Michigan.

All of these Dream Car line illustrations were produced on Macintosh computer by enthusiast Bob Eng of Torrance, California.

1951 Buick XP-300 *Drawing by Bob Eng*

1952–53 Corvette *Drawing by Bob Eng*

1953 Pontiac Parisienne

1953 Pontiac Parisienne *Drawing by Bob Eng*

1953 Oldsmobile Starfire

1953 Oldsmobile Starfire
Drawing by Bob Eng

1953 Buick Wildcat

1953 Buick Wildcat I *Drawing by Bob Eng*

1953 LeMans

1953 Cadillac LeMans *Drawing by Bob Eng*

1953 Cadillac Orleans

1953 Cadillac Orleans *Drawing by Bob Eng*

1954 XP-21 Firebird

1954 Firebird I *Drawing by Bob Eng*

1954 Nomad

1954 Corvette Nomad *Drawing by Bob Eng*

1954 Corvair

1954 Corvair Fastback *Drawing by Bob Eng*

1954 Pontiac Strato Streak *Drawing by Bob Eng*

1954 Pontiac Bonneville Special *Drawing by Bob Eng*

1954 Olds F-88 *Drawing by Bob Eng*

1954 Olds Cutlass *Drawing by Bob Eng*

1954 Buick Wildcat II

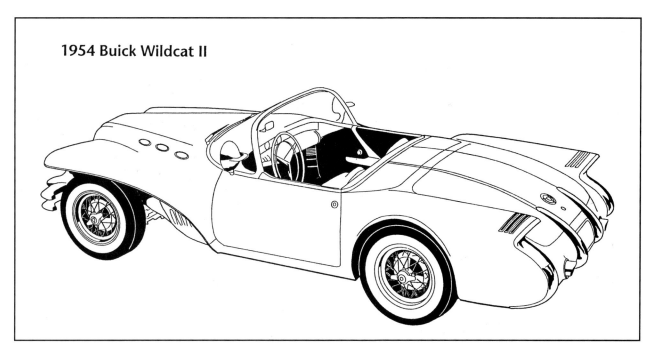

1954 Buick Wildcat II *Drawing by Bob Eng*

1954 Park Avenue

1954 Cadillac Park Avenue *Drawing by Bob Eng*

1954 Cadillac La Espada

1954 Cadillac La Espada *Drawing by Bob Eng*

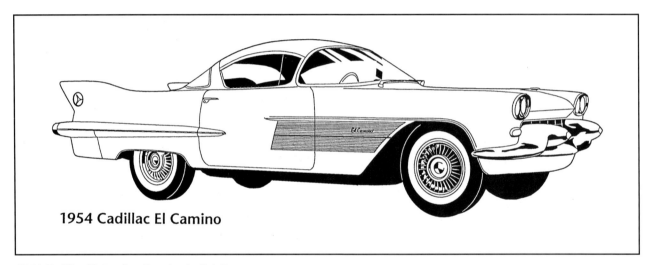

1954 Cadillac El Camino

1954 Cadillac El Camino *Drawing by Bob Eng*

1955 L'Universelle

1955 GMC L'Universelle *Drawing by Bob Eng*

1955 Chevrolet Biscayne *Drawing by Bob Eng*

1955 Pontiac Strato-Star *Drawing by Bob Eng*

1955 Olds 88 Delta *Drawing by Bob Eng*

1955 Buick Wildcat III *Drawing by Bob Eng*

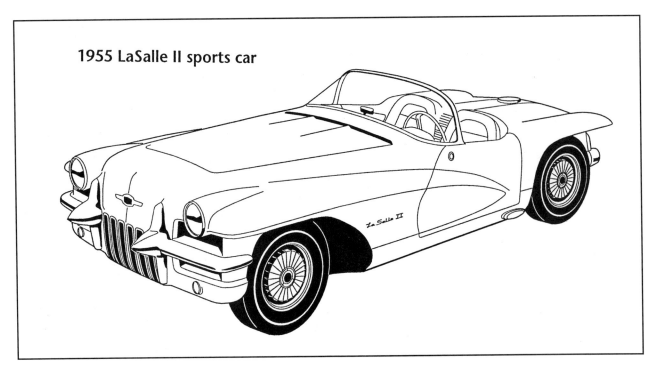

1955 LaSalle II Roadster *Drawing by Bob Eng*

1955 LaSalle II Four-Door *Drawing by Bob Eng*

1955 Eldorado Brougham

1955 Cadillac Eldorado Brougham *Drawing by Bob Eng*

1956 Firebird II

1956 Firebird II *Drawing by Bob Eng*

1956 Chevrolet Impala *Drawing by Bob Eng*

1956 Pontiac Club De Mer *Drawing by Bob Eng*

1956 Oldsmobile Golden Rocket *Drawing by Bob Eng*

1956 Buick Centurion *Drawing by Bob Eng*

1956 Eldorado Brougham Town Car

1956 Cadillac Eldorado Brougham Town Car
Drawing by Bob Eng

1959 Firebird III

1959 Firebird III *Drawing by Bob Eng*

1959 Cadillac Cyclone

Bob Eng

1959 Cadillac Cyclone *Drawing by Bob Eng*

Index